TOWARDS A
SOCIOLOGY OF MANAGEMENT

ALSO BY SIR GEOFFREY VICKERS

The Art of Judgment (1965)
The Undirected Society (1959)

Towards a
Sociology of Management

SIR GEOFFREY VICKERS

BASIC BOOKS, INC., PUBLISHERS

New York

Contents

Foreword

THE PAPERS collected here originated on various occasions, usually as talks to administrators or business men intent on exploring the nature of what they were doing. The unity which, I hope, justifies their being thus assembled derives from their common viewpoint. They all start from and try to illuminate the belief that business is a social activity and management a form of social regulation. They all use, as their main clues to understanding, two sets of concepts which have not yet fully permeated thinking or practice. One set is derived from general systems theory; the other from communication science.

The first theme stresses the importance of the circular process of control, with its endless comparison of 'what is' with 'what ought to be'; a process exemplified by cybernetic assemblies but familiar in all systems, biological, psychological and social. But it stresses equally the fact that in the management of human organizations, feedback is often absent, ambiguous or uninformative and points to the complementary processes of mental simulation which enable management to function in such conditions.

The second theme stresses the part played by human expectations, socially generated, in setting and changing the manifold and often conflicting standards of what 'ought to be' – the standards of success – and hence in determining and constantly altering the 'states' which human organizations are set to seek. It is thus concerned with the social process by which these conventional standards are set and changed and with the part which management should take in that process. For management is properly and inescapably concerned to set and change its standards of success, as well as to attain them.

The main effect of this approach is to identify a basic difference which

9

seems to distinguish psycho-social systems from other kinds of open system. A subsidiary effect is to mute the difference which sociologists are wont to draw, within human systems, between the 'artificial' organizations of business and the 'natural' societies of men; still more, the even more unreal distinction which the mythology of capitalism draws between 'profit-making' and 'non-profit-making' undertakings; and to stress the conventional nature of those standards of success by which all alike are activated and which are generated by the very process which they regulate.

Since most of these papers were written, I have tried to distill into a book[1] the main ideas which pervade them; but it may be that these will be more easily assimiable in the form of successive approximations from different angles, than as one articulated whole. I hope that, taken together, they may make some contribution towards that important and still rudimentary branch of knowledge, the sociology of management.

Chapters 5 and 6 are new, though they originated in unscripted talks given in 1966 at the School of Business and Public Administration in the University of Missouri at Kansas City and in the London Graduate School of Business Studies. The others, in form only slightly different from those which appear here, have been published in *The Manager* (chs. 1, 4 and 12); the *Journal of Industrial Economics* (ch. 2); *Occupational Psychology* (ch. 3); the *Political Quarterly* (ch. 8); and the *Journal of the British Institute of Industrial Administration* (ch. 11). Chapter 7, the ninth Wallberg Lecture, was separately published by the University of Toronto Press; chapter 10 by Tavistock Publications. Chapter 9 appeared in the proceedings of a conference on the impact of automation organized by the Government of Ontario and published by it in Toronto in 1964. Chapter 10 appeared also in the proceedings of the seventeenth annual meeting of the World Federation for Mental Health. Chapter 12 was also published in a slightly shortened form in *The Lancet*. For permission to republish chapters 7 and 9, I am indebted respectively to the Faculty of Applied Science and Engineering of the University of

[1] *The Art of Judgment.* (1965) London: Chapman and Hall, and New York: Basic Books Inc.

Toronto and to the Government of Ontario, as well as to the publishers already mentioned. I have included the last paper, although written more than ten years ago, because, unhappily, time has neither changed the character nor abated the urgency of the situations with which it deals.

Goring-on-Thames
England
May 1967

PART ONE

CHAPTER ONE

Cybernetics and the Management of Men*

ENGINEERS make machines which control themselves and each other. These machines 'appreciate the situation', measure the divergence of what is from what ought to be and adapt their behaviour accordingly. In doing so, they apply 'rules' which they have previously learned; and some, in the absence of an appropriate rule, will find one and remember it next time.

In all this they behave very much like men, who they excel in accuracy though not in variety of response.

Such machines do not need to be continually 'directed', like a chisel or a lathe or a bus. They do not even have to be continually supervised. They will do these things largely for themselves. The job of the engineer is to maintain them in optimum condition and to define from time to time what they are expected to do.

Now this is precisely the goal of all managers of men. How simple life would be if management, having defined the common purpose, could confine itself to the care of health, welfare and working conditions, leaving the organization to run itself! This also is the goal of all the managed. Who would ask more than to be given the general objective and allowed to get on with the job, self-directed and self-controlled, in working conditions as favourable as single-minded attention could make them? The automatic factory is a model to the 'directed' factory not merely in efficiency but also in what for lack of a better word we might call 'ideology'.

It used to be a reproach to a manager that he treated men like machines. We may be in sight of the day when it is a reproach to the

*An address given at the annual conference of the British Institute of Management in 1955.

engineer that he has to treat machines like men. In the brave new world of automation we may hear one engineer say to another:

> That is an inefficient and out-moded machine, almost as unreliable as a man. You have to be always telling it what to do and even then you never know whether it will do it.

To all this, of course, the managers of men could make forceful replies. Men are not much more like AA gun predictors or homing missiles than they are like hand-operated lathes. This may well be true; but my concern in this paper is to see what managers of men can learn from the principles which engineers are evolving for the control of machines. These principles may be of only limited application in controlling organizations of men, but in this field any help is welcome; and we may learn as much from differences as from similarities.

Feedback plays a central part in the engineer's idea of control. Whenever purposeful action is being taken, it can best be checked by comparing its result with the result it is intended to produce. Is it having the desired effect? If not, in what way and to what extent is the result deviating from what was purposed? This deviation is the measure of the action needed to correct it. If the deviation can be made to operate a mechanism which will 'automatically' modify future action in the way needed to correct the error, then the circuit is closed and the system is set to control itself.

There are several essential elements in this circuit, *i.e.*,

(1) *Prediction.* We must be able to predict at every stage what effect the action ought to have if it is to produce the desired result.

(2) *Information.* We must know what effect the action is actually having.

(3) *Measurement.* We must be able to measure the difference between what is and what ought to be at least sufficiently for the next steps.

(4) *Coding and communication.* The measured deviation must be coded in some convenient form and transmitted to the centre, or centres, from which action can be taken.

(5) *Response.* This signal must elicit infallibly and at once the action needed to compensate for the deviation. Where different situations may call for different responses, there must also be a selecting mechanism which will choose the appropriate response; perhaps even a mechanism which will search for

the right response by trial and error, discarding each solution which proves unsatisfactory by some predetermined rule.

(6) *Co-ordination.* Where the response evoked is complex, its various parts must be co-ordinated. This may require further feedback circuits between the different parts of the responding machine.

In devising controlled systems the engineer has two main problems. He has to devise indices which will reflect with sufficient exactness the changing value of critical variables; and he has to arrange for these to trigger off appropriate compensating action. In both fields he has great scope for inventive skill.

Now all this is true also of the manager. He, too, needs indices which will measure and record the deviation from the appointed path. He, too, needs to devise means by which the recorded deviation will of itself initiate compensating action at many levels and to see that this is co-ordinated so as not to defeat itself. He, too, needs to recognize – and needs that all at the appropriate levels of action shall be able to recognize – which of several possible lines of action is called for and to know when to discard one as unsuccessful. And in all this he, too, has need and scope for great inventive skill in devising techniques to meet his needs.

He has, however, peculiar difficulties. Consider the field of prediction, information and measurement. The principle of control by budget and forecast is now widely accepted in principle, though by no means applied in practice as widely as it can be. There has been a great advance in accounting and statistical techniques to serve this need. The use of standard costs promises an advance in signalling deviations between what is and what ought to be to the levels where the information is needed.

There remain, however, important fields where this basic measurement is lacking and perhaps is unobtainable. I know, for example, of no reliable method of measuring the result of a training programme and comparing it with a reliable forecast of what it ought to be. Here as elsewhere the difficulty is largely due to the number of variables, some unidentified, which are operating at the same time.

For there must be economy of indices. No technician can watch more than a certain number of dials; no manager can observe and collate more than a certain number of usually less obvious signals. The engineer is ingenious in identifying key indices, in devising analogues, in shunting the work of comparing and collating on to other machines. The manager in his wider and more difficult field begins to show the same initiative; but he has a long way to go.

Next, the signal has to reach the place from which action can be taken. Here the manager's problem is notably more complicated than that of the engineer. Where the deviation from course strikes directly on the attention of those whose action is sufficient to put things right, control will usually take care of itself. But as organizations grow larger and their purposes become wider in scope and longer in term, this state of affairs becomes ever more rare. Usually the problem presents itself in one of two forms.

Sometimes the problem presents itself at the working level but requires action at headquarters. Sometimes it presents itself at headquarters but requires action on the shop floor. In either case the problem is the same – how to make A respond to a stimulus received by B? It is sometimes supposed that this is merely a question of communicating the facts to all concerned. This is, I think, too simple a view. All are not set and cannot be set to respond in the same way to the same facts. This ideal might often be realized more fully than it is now but it cannot bridge the whole gap. In addition, the signal on its way up and down must be translated – recoded, if you like – into a form to which the receiving level is accustomed to respond.

When we come to the selection of appropriate action, the problems of the manager diverge still further from those of the engineer. The thermostat, if moved to act at all, has only two answers – to increase or to reduce the draught. The answers available to a board of directors, a manager, even a foreman, are usually more numerous than this, even though they are in practice more limited than the outside observer would suppose. Moreover, the choice between action and inaction – often the most critical choice of all – is far more complicated. There are also decisions of timing. So, generally speaking, when a board of directors behaves with the rigidly determined responses of a thermostat – as boards of directors often do, especially in financial matters – it is either a reflection on their powers of decision or a sign that they have got into such a jam, that choice is no longer open to them.

Finally, it remains to consider the fact that, while engineers are concerned with physical and chemical interactions, managers are concerned with the interactions of men. This, you may say, means that the analogy between mechanical and human systems breaks down completely at the last stage, namely the stage of action. The task of eliciting a response from a machine is different in kind from that of eliciting a response from a man.

If we were to discuss how far this is true, we should get into philosophical depths too great for the time at our disposal or for the occasion. Let us assume, then, that it is completely true. The analogy still serves to crystallize in the clearest way the fundamental problems of the manager of men. If the last stage has its own peculiar difficulties, the analysis is none the less useful.

I have time to draw only a few conclusions.

First, I commend to you the basic idea that action should be controlled by the observed difference between what is and what ought to be. This, I agree, should be obvious enough; yet it requires of a manager powers of objectivity as well as of observation which are still rare. I remember the comment of a wise and successful man of affairs on the behaviour of a well-known public figure. He said:

> With X the knowledge that something is wrong provokes an ungovernable desire to act. This produces action; and this in turn relieves the urge. The cycle is completed and he feels satisfied, irrespective of what the result may be. The next stimulus will send him off on another cycle of action; but he won't ask himself whether it was caused by his own wrong action last time. He is never at a loss what to do; sometimes he even does the right thing; but he is not himself controlled by results so he cannot be a controller.

This is a devastating criticism but one which it is all too easy to merit. Let us hope that the spread of cybernetic ideas may build up our standards of what to expect in this respect from each other and even from ourselves.

Next, I commend to you the idea that control is mutual. This opens the door to a better understanding of control and one which is badly needed; for in my experience this word is at present almost unusable, so many are its meanings and so explosive its connotations. This is partly because our language, unlike French or German, does not clearly distinguish between control and direction; but chiefly because industry is still haunted by ways of thinking which are formed on the model of 'open-circuit' rather than 'closed-circuit' methods of mechanical control, that is, by the idea of one-way rather than two-way relationships. We may have got beyond the stage when foremen told workmen that they were not paid to think; but we are still far from accepting the need for feedback throughout the chain of command; and even where it is accepted that this should carry information upwards as well as carrying orders downwards, the difference between an order and a piece of information tends to be exaggerated.

Control does not mean the exercise of power by A over B. Indeed, where this is needed, it is evidence that control is imperfect. The better the organization works, the less such incursions of power are required. Ideally, control is mediated not by power but by information; and this information flows up, down and sideways within a well-running organization and its effect depends on its relevance, not on its source. Responsibilities are structured but control is mutual. This is a concept which has been put forward for decades by the insight of humane writers on management – it is, for example, what Mary Parker Follett was saying thirty years ago – and I count it a great good that it should be endorsed by a desiccated science completely devoid of ethical overtones.

Again, I find that the diseases of mechanical control systems throw much light on the diseases of human organizations. Thus control systems are prone to oscillate; and this is due to some defect in the organization of feedback. Sometimes it is too sluggish, so that the correction comes too late. Sometimes it is too sensitive, so that the correction is too violent. Sometimes it is not sufficiently selective, so that disturbances are transmitted to parts of the assembly which cannot usefully deal with them. All these diseases have close parallels in the diseases of organizations. I would particularly stress the last, for I believe that the first impact of these ideas on human organization has been to promote the uncritical multiplication of feedback circuits in the belief that you cannot have too much of a good thing. This I believe to be a mistake.

Finally, I commend to your attention the thought that control is ubiquitous. The engineers, by devising control systems, have made clearer to us the principles which govern the interaction of parts within wholes, whether the wholes be machines, men or societies. There are great differences between assemblies of men, assemblies of cells and assemblies of mechanical or electronic components; but none of these assemblies hangs together except by virtue of a balance of forces such that any change in one variable evokes compensating changes in others sufficient to maintain the essential conditions of stability. Each of us is a hierarchy of systems; our present activities and our long-term purposes depend alike on scores of physiological mechanisms, each devoted to maintaining some essential variable – our temperature, our blood sugar and so on – within the narrow limits on which consciousness and life depend; and an organization is an even greater complexity of system piled on system. Our consciously planned controls are intruders in a tissue of interaction in which an immense number of unconscious controls are already at work.

Science can tell us something and will tell us more about the laws which govern the interaction of systems. In the meantime it is, I think, a great help to view an organization as a system of systems, each of which is self-controlled and seeks, often unconsciously, its own stability. A familiar example is the resistance to change with which lower formations so often meet the best laid plans of top management – or for that matter with which top management so often meets such signals as reach them from the lower deck.

The theory of control is, in fact, an approach to the understanding of the laws which make it possible for wholes to cohere and to act coherently. These laws have long been fundamental to physiology; they are opening the door to the design of coherent assemblies of machines. At the other extreme they are increasingly used in economic analysis; an electrical engineer has written a book on *The Mechanism of Economic Systems.*[1] In the field of social organization with which managers are concerned they are less well understood and less well applied, though the work of Kurt Lewin and others offers much and promises more. I believe that science is already offering to the managers of men a means to order and extend their intuitive knowledge to an extent of which few are aware and that during the next few decades it will illumine their empirical art with dazzling light. It is time to begin adjusting our eyes to the new level of illumination.

Let me conclude with a parable.

There was once a company which owned a dance hall. The directors asked an engineer to design a heating system which would maintain a constant temperature in the hall, whatever the vagaries of the weather or of the heat generated by their clients' activities; and the engineer put a thermostat in the hall and connected it in the usual way with the boiler in the boiler house, so as to vary the draught according to the heat of the hall.

Well, this system began to work very badly, so the directors called in the designer. He found that some odd things had happened.

First, the coal-cellar, alarmed at the rate at which it had to release coal when the boiler opened up, had devised a subsidiary system, whereby the draught door was made responsive to the amount of coal in the coal-cellar. When the cellar was only half full, the draught door would not open more than half-way, whatever the thermostat said – and so on. This made sure that whatever happened to the boiler or the ballroom, the coal-cellar at all events would never be empty. (I have known financial controls which functioned very much like that.)

The boiler also had views of its own. It liked to keep its water jacket at a constant temperature and it hated continually hotting up and cooling down to compensate for what was happening in the ballroom. So it devised a system by which the draught could not be increased or diminished by more than was consistent with keeping the water jacket at a constant heat. It decided, in fact, to look after its own stability first, as people at the working level often do.

The designer had a meeting with the coal-cellar and the boiler. Being an expert in cybernetics, he did not begin by upbraiding them for not accepting the common purpose. He asked them what was the matter. He soon realized that it was asking too much of any coal-cellar to let its coal run out to the last knob without knowing when the next lot was coming: and that the wear and tear on the boiler really was rather heavy. So he got the coal-cellar to agree that its private control should not operate until the cellar was half-empty; and he gave an undertaking that he would always refill by then. And he got the boiler to co-operate on condition that he built into the main control a delay action, which limited the rate at which it could be required to change temperature. This met all requirements and produced a more refined system than before.

So they started it up again; but it still did not work.

The designer went over it all again. It was perfect; but it was being bedevilled by a system of quite another kind.

The night watchman spent the night in the boiler room; and he hated draughts. So he filled up every crevice with newspaper. The draught door could open as much as it liked; there was no air intake to the room.

Well, that was easy. The designer put in a system of ducts which delivered air to the boiler without cooling the night watchman's feet and thus uncoupled the heating system from the system of the night watchman, with which it had inadvertently become entangled. Then he started the boiler up again.

The system still did not work.

The directors then lost patience with the scientist and called in a builder, who pointed out that the chimney was full of starlings' nests. A chimney-sweep removed these and the system has worked like a charm ever since. The sweep got all the credit, which is a pity, because, in fact, all the starlings' nests were built while the ducts were being put in and had nothing to do with the real trouble at all. Any one acquanited with the habits of starlings could have told the directors this, but by now they were not interested in the scientific approach. Even the scientific member of the board dare not suggest that they should call in an ornithologist.

This parable has perhaps too many morals. In each case the trouble was a conflict of systems; but the first two were different from the last two. The first two were conflicts within the system itself. They arose because the system did not take sufficient account of the needs of a subordinate system and they were resolved by incorporating what was needed to do so. The second two were conflicts between the system and other systems which had no necessary connection with it. All that was needed here was to disentangle the two. And even here the difference in method is worth noting. The night watchman was accommodated in a way which found a use for the residual heat of the boiler; the starlings were simply sent elsewhere. In a world which is getting so very crowded the first is likely to be preferred increasingly to the second.

Maybe this is the most important implication of all. It is natural that those responsible for maintaining a system should seek to do so first by isolating it forcibly from all those outside it and by unifying it forcibly within; but in the long run this is not practicable. Our world is becoming too interconnected. It is possible, then, that a better understanding of these laws of interaction may provide a firm basis for rules of conduct which at present rest only on ethical intuition; but that is a speculation too far-reaching to be supported by a parable.

REFERENCE

[1] Tustin, A. *The Mechanism of Economic Systems.* (1953) London: Heinemann.

CHAPTER TWO

Positive and Negative Controls in Business

I USE the word 'control' throughout this paper in an exact and rather narrow sense. By a control I intend a means of comparing any state, actual or hypothetical, with a standard. The building contractor plots on charts against time the projected course of many interdependent operations; and against these courses he plots, week by week, the progress actually achieved. Thus he is able continually to compare what is with what ought to be; and this is the essence of control.

Some of the standards which the contractor plots are limits which must not be transgressed. Others will give cause for concern if the actual diverges from the standard in either direction. It does not matter, for example, how quickly planning permission is obtained, so long as it is obtained before he wants to begin to build; but it does matter if one phase of building is completed so much ahead of time that the labour cannot be at once deployed on the next phase. The first type of control I refer to as negative control and I call the standard a limit. The second I refer to as positive control and I call the standard a norm.

When performance transgresses a limit or diverges from a norm, the damage which ensues varies with the amount of the divergence but not in any constant way. Within certain limits it may be negligible. Thereafter, the damage may be acute at first and may then accrue more slowly; or (more usually) it may accrue at an accelerating rate. In either case, there is likely to come a point beyond which dramatic and irreversible changes occur. For example, shortage of cash causes progressive embarrassment, as it becomes more acute; but if it reaches the point at which the bank refuses to meet the weekly wages cheque, its effect suddenly overflows and brings the whole operation to a standstill. Beyond each limit and on either side of each norm there usually exist points such as this, which cannot be passed without effecting radical and irreversible change. These points of no return I call thresholds.

I invite you then to regard a business and the processes which compose it as a system of variables, which can maintain itself only so long as the values and mutual relations of the variables are kept within certain thresholds. Within these limits management at all levels operates. When management can compare what is happening with standards defining what should or should not be happening if its plans are to be realized, it is exercising control.

The comparison of the actual with the standard (be it norm or limit) gives a signal, conveniently called a 'mis-match' signal. If control is to be effective, this signal has to release the right sort of action, that is, action which will bring the situation back towards the norm or away from the limit. Often, at least in English, the word control covers the remedial action as well as the eliciting of the signal. Sometimes it is used simply of the remedial action. For example, a skidding car is said to be out of control, whether the driver realizes all too well the difference between what is and what ought to be or whether he is too drunk to know that anything is the matter. In French and German the corresponding word is kept much more carefully for the sense in which I am using it and this is desirable, especially when we are talking about the kind of controls which I have in mind. If we were talking only about thermostats and safety valves – equally, examples of positive and negative controls – the distinction would not be important, for the way in which a thermostat or a safety valve recognizes deviation from a norm or arrival at a limit is inseparable from the remedial action which it takes. But with the controls which I have in mind, the question – 'What is the position?' is distinct from the question – 'What do we do about it?' and we must have separate words for them. I am keeping the word control for the first half of the process.

The deviation which a control registers has a time dimension. The building contractor is concerned to know not merely that an operation is x days behind schedule but also that it is running y per cent more slowly than schedule. The rate at which it is deviating from a norm or approaching a limit is at least as important as the amount of the current deviation or the current safety margin as the case may be.

I do not apologize for beginning with this careful and arid definition of terms, for the word control is one of the most confused words in the English language and in business it has collected so many emotional overtones that in some quarters it is hardly usable. Yet it is fundamental to management whether of money, materials, processes or men. It is equally essential to the idea of self-control and hence to all discussion of decentralization.

Control serves three different purposes. It provides means to compare performance (a) with norms and limits which are given by the nature of the operation, (b) with forecasts reflecting the expected results of policies, and (c) with targets representing goals for attainment. The first shows whether the system is approaching an objectively defined limit, for example, exhaustion of cash resources or moving favourably or otherwise according to objectively defined indices of efficiency such as profitability or rate of turnover. The second shows whether the system is following the course forecast as most probable on the basis of its policy and thus checks whether current plans are being realized and provides a basis for future planning. The third provides a measure of success.

The second and third differ in that they use slightly different norms and limits. For most planning purposes the estimate should be as realistic as possible, that is, it should be as likely to be too high as too low. Sometimes, for example, for controlling the margin of cash resources and in other controls related to thresholds, it should be extremely conservative. By contrast, where the standard is used as a standard of success, it should be as high as will give a reasonable chance of its being attained. It is thus seldom possible to make one set of standards serve both purposes.

This difficulty is accentuated by two factors which today are more troublesome than they need be. The first is the tendency for standards to become too precise. It is seldom possible to estimate what should be, without a large margin of error. These margins tend to disappear on paper and there is always a danger that the resultant figure will acquire a sanctity which it does not deserve, the assumptions on which it is based being forgotten.

This difficulty is partly technical. It is easy to express estimates as a figure with a margin of error. It is inconvenient to aggregate margins of error but it is not impossible; simple mathematical techniques are available. It would be welcome, if accountants would devise acceptably simple methods of preserving margins of error in our estimates. Meantime, it is not surprising that business men often prefer to derive norms and limits from their inner consciousness, rather than allow themselves to be forced into the unreal rigidity of a figure.

If all standards could be represented as bands, rather than as precise figures, this difficulty would disappear and it would become easier to use the same standards for target and for forecast. The top of the bracket would represent the target, the mean would be the forecast and the bottom would be the threshold.

The second difficulty springs from the need to include in forecasts an allowance for uncontrollable contingencies, whilst targets for success need to be related as closely as may be to factors under the control of the authority whose success is to be measured. These allowances can of course be distinguished within the composition of the standard; but the larger they bulk, the harder it becomes to reconcile effectively the standards of forecast and target.

The virtue of formalizing control in this way is that it makes the standards of comparison precise and explicit. It thus ensures that they shall be formulated with due care. It reveals inconsistencies between one standard and another and between the standards of one user and another. It makes standards public and fosters common and realistic views of what is, and common and realistic expectations of what should be. These are benefits of the greatest value. To secure them is a major responsibility of management.

The main dangers of control, as we at present know it, are that it is liable to focus attention too exclusively on fields where control can be established; to magnify errors which are built in to the control system itself; and to withdraw awareness from the wide and important fields where action is not in fact controllable.

Control is used to guide action. It must therefore be available at each level where action is taken and the guidance it supplies at each level must be relevant to the action which is taken *at that level*.

Control systems are often more elaborate at higher than at lower levels of an organization. The only justification for this – and it is at best an inadequate and partial one – is that higher levels are blind without organized controls, whilst lower levels are more directly aware of what is going on. There is in fact no level, not even the individual level, at which we are aware of *all* that is going on. Selection is involved even in individual perception. At every level we have to choose what indices to watch and it is useful to make the choice explicit.

Furthermore, remedial action depends largely on people at each action level being directly aware of what is going wrong and hence of what is required of them. They should need direction from a level above only when the action required is related to some situation which can only be seen from the level above – as when the overall financial position of the undertaking limits what would otherwise be appropriate action by one section of it.

In a large organization it is necessary and proper to insist that indices which need to be recorded and used centrally, are recorded and used in the same way at lower levels. Given this, it should scarcely ever occur that information required at a higher level has not already been collected and examined at a lower level or that an inquiry arising at a higher level has not already been asked and answered at a lower level. The only proper exceptions are those rare ones when the information sought is only relevant when it has been aggregated. With this sole exception, if a lower level has to prepare information or answer questions specially at the request of a higher level, the fact is itself prima facie evidence that the lower level has neglected its job or that the higher level has asked an irrelevant question.

Generally speaking, the indices of control become less significant and less useful at progressively higher levels. At every aggregation, significance is lost. Control at any level cannot be more effective than it is at the levels below. If top management can ensure adequate control at operating levels, control at higher levels will present no difficulties.

Since the 'lowest' – and thus the most important – 'level' is the individual, it is worthy of note that these foregoing principles apply equally to the self-control of the individual, both generally and in the doing of his job in business. Individuals also control their own behaviour by comparing its results with positive and negative standards (norms and limits) which they have somehow established. Ineffective human conduct is more often due to deviance in the setting of the norms and limits (the 'ought to be' and the 'ought not to be') or to failure to appreciate the relevant situation (the 'is') than to inability to act on the mis-match signal. It follows that the effective control of a business depends absolutely (amongst other things) on the ability of each individual man and woman in it to recognize what the situation requires of him or her and to act accordingly.

Not all action is 'controllable'. The more important it is, the less controllable it is likely to be. This is, unhappily, inherent in the nature of control.

The helmsman derives from the compass card a continuous stream of signals, showing the divergence of the ship's head from the appointed course. His response is expressed in a movement of the rudder within seconds after he receives the visual signal; and the result of the rudder movement is fed back to him, again within seconds, by the further movement of the ship's head, reflected in the compass. Conditions of control are thus almost optimal. Yet even in this brief time-lag many effects of wind and sea, some of them more potent than the rudder, have added their quota to the movement of the ship's head. What the helmsman sees, in the movement of the ship's head, is not the result of his helm movements alone but the result of many forces, of which his helm movements are only one. He gets sufficient guidance to steer by only because most of these other forces are fairly regular and of those which are not – such as an exceptional sea on the bow – he is usually directly aware.

In the control of human affairs, information about the current position and current trends is usually intermittent, partial and sometimes greatly in arrear, whilst the results of our responses may not return for judgment for months or years; by which time they may have become mixed with many more potent variables, perhaps unpredictable or even unknown and may furnish neither validation of the past nor guide for the future. The field of control is strictly limited.

It is important therefore – (a) to extend the field of control as widely as may be; (b) to recognize its limitations; (c) to undetrand the principles of action outside the field of control and to have the courage to act on them.

The field of control is limited primarily by the length of time which elapses before the results of action return for judgment and by the nature of variables which by that time have intervened to mask its results.

Within these general limitations, it is limited further by the degree of precision with which we can measure the actual and define the standard with which the actual should be compared.

Whether the conditions of control exist or not, human behaviour, whether in business or out of it, is basically rule-governed. It is guided by applying to the situation, as perceived, rules which take one of two forms. They may take the form – 'To achieve this, do that' or – 'To avoid this, do that'. Alternatively, they may take the more general form 'In these circumstances, do this'; or 'In these circumstances, avoid doing that'. Since whatever we do has far more effects than we intend or can foresee, we act on rules of the second more general pattern more often and more justifiably than we realize.

When the conditions of control are present, we can check the results of our rule-governed behaviour and revise our rules or the application of them – or, more probably, our view of the situation in which we are acting – in accordance with our experience. This is of the greatest value, the more so because the conditions of control are so often not present.

Moreover, the existence of control, even in a limited field, reminds us that all action is tentative, based on assumptions which may prove to be mistaken. This helps to prevent us becoming more blind than we need be.

It is equally important that the use of controls, where they are available, should not spoil our nerve or our skill in those more numerous and more important situations where decisions must be taken at times when we are denied the reassurance of control, either because the feedback is too slow to be useful or because 'bad visibility' obscures the actual or the norm or both.

CHAPTER THREE

The Role of Expectation in Economic Systems*

I INVITE you to regard as the prototype of an economic system one of those biological communities which ecologists like to study; a community within an area in which a characteristic set of conditions is sharply isolated, such as a rain forest or pond. Such a community is entitled to be called a system because of its capacity for self-regulation. And we can call it an economic system, because the aspects which we study relate to the way in which the creatures composing it maintain themselves and multiply. We can regard it as a complex of biochemical factories, continuously engaged in meeting their own and each other's needs.

Within such a system is a hierarchy of sub-systems. We can distinguish groups of organisms, each linked by so close a net of mutual relationships that it can usefully be regarded as a system. These vary in degree, from the roughly systematic relations between a population of predators and its prey to the almost organic interaction of a colony of social insects. And within these subordinate systems, each individual organism is a system in its own right. All these systems are open systems, maintaining themselves by exchanging matter with their environments at a rate dictated by their metabolic needs and in ways resulting from the manifold interaction of their individual capacities for behaviour. And each of them, like every open system, continues only so long as it can maintain within acceptable limits the external relationships by which it lives and the internal relationships by which it hangs together. Every open system is the expression of a double dynamic balance, internal and external, these being two adjacent levels in the hierarchy

*A paper given at the annual conference of the British Psychological Society in 1958.

of relatedness.

When we raise our eyes from the rain forest and the pond to observe the sterling area or I.C.I. or the individuals debouching from the 8.45 at Liverpool Street, we find a scene basically familiar but changed in important respects. One notable change is the immense proliferation of intermediate systems, deliberately organized. The individual business undertaking is a system. Externally, it must exchange with its environment goods and services, money and men on such terms as at least to make good its losses. Internally, it must maintain such relationships between its members as will secure their effective co-operation. But here, as in the rain forest and the pond, the dynamism is supplied by the seekings and shunnings of individual creatures; and the economist like the ecologist, as he studies the regularities, the oscillations, the correlations of systems above the level of the organism, is always reaching frontiers beyond which he cannot pass without asking, 'What regulates the behaviour of the individual?' And this is a psychological question.

I am to discuss one of these regulators, the regulator called expectation. It plays a conscious part in the regulation of economic systems but it is not, of course, peculiar to them. On the contrary, it is a basic regulator of human behaviour and therefore of psychological interest in its own right, more particularly because, as it seems to me, psychological theory has not yet paid it sufficient attention. To some extent it also governs the behaviour of non-human organisms; but at the human level it seems to assume a peculiar measure of importance.

The direction and control of a business at the conscious level is based on maintaining and continually comparing two running representations of what is going to happen next. One is a representation of the actual, the other of the intended. Thus the building contractor plots on charts against time the intended course of many interdependent operations; and, as work proceeds, he plots against these the results which are actually being realized and projects these also into the future so far as he can. Any divergence of the actual from the intended is a signal, first for enquiry and then for action designed to bring the actual into

34

line with the intended; or, if this proves impossible, to alter the plan so as to produce an attainable governing course. There is a continual two-way interchange between the two sets of expectations, as those in charge mould the future course of events to match their intentions or modify their intentions to take account of the future course of events. Sometimes one is dominant and sometimes the other.

Such controls may be positive or negative. A positive control is signalled by the divergence of the actual from some norm, such as a short-fall in planned production. Negative control is signalled by the approach of the actual to some limit which we regard as unacceptable – such as the limit of our overdraft facilities. There are, incidentally, important differences between the operation of positive and negative control and I believe that negative control is the more common, not least in business. I suggest, therefore, that psychology has done a disservice to lay thought – perhaps even to its own – by talking of goal seeking as if it comprised all purposive behaviour; and that economists forget how often men in business are motivated by fear rather than by greed.

In any case, neither positive nor negative control would give adequate guidance, unless both the actual and the intended (or the feared) could be projected into the future.

Such controls, positive and negative, also govern those internal activities of a firm which are directed to securing through time enough of the right men of the right level – activities which include its policies of selection, recruitment, training, education, promotion and staff development. The firm knows what it wants and what it must avoid and against these standards it continually compares its actual and unfolding achievement – sometimes unconsciously and in general but often explicitly and in detail. Its adaptive behaviour is geared to the resulting mis-match signals.

When I speak of comparing the actual with the intended – or with the feared – I simplify the process in what may be a dangerous way. What we actually compare are two representations similarly coded, be it in words or figures or graphically – how else could we compare them? The actual cannot be more than a representation of some aspects of what we think is in course of occurring. It is selective; it is hypothetical;

it has an inescapable time dimension and in representing change-with-time, it is as much at home in the future as in the past. Further, it is represented in a symbolism which limits and distorts it in many ways which we can recognize. Thus the 'actual' and the 'intended' are constructs of the same kind. These considerations, I suggest, apply with equal force to the mental processes by which the individual mind compares the actual with the intended. For it, also, the actual, no less than the intended, is selective, hypothetical, extended in time and rendered in a symbolism which may limit and distort it in ways still unknown. But I will defer the consideration of these psychological implications until the end of the paper.

I want first to focus the familiar fact that the conscious representation of the expected plays an important part in the conduct of business – that is, in the way in which systems of the kind we are considering today maintain both their inner coherence and their relation with the environment. Policy making and executive decision and the continuous process of control within which these decisions are taken depend on the power to build hypothetical models of future events and to respond to these models. Collectively and individually, we constantly maintain and continually revise our inner representation of the environment and of our relation with it – or rather those aspects of it to which we think it worth while to attend – and our responses are governed not directly by what is happening 'out there' but by changes in these inner representations.

The part played by expectation in the regulation of our behaviour, in business as elsewhere, is, of course, much more ubiquitous and less conscious than this. Our conscious expectations are built on assumptions on which we have come unconsciously to rely but which are no less expectations. That our customers will pay their bills, our suppliers will keep their contracts, are expectations which form part of our basic set of assumptions. We can sometimes attach to them degrees of probability of considerable refinement but we cannot do business unless the degree of probability is fairly high. Some of these assumptions are essential to the working of the system – for example, the assumption that banks will remain solvent. This is an 'on or off' phenomenon; any position other than complete trust brings to an end all business which depends on the bank or banks concerned. By contrast, our expectations regarding inflation approach a threshold more gradually. Business can continue in the expectation of a continuing moderate rate of inflation, though this introduces elements of instability; for example, it leads to overstocking, which in turn leads to an unreal expansion of activity, which in turn contributes to the inflationary spiral. But in time a point is reached when the system breaks down, either because the rate of change in the value of money is too rapid to be accommodated within the time scale of business operations or because sheer uncertainty removes the basis for action. No business system can survive in the inflationary conditions in the Germany of 1924.

These expectations affect the situations to which they relate. Whether a trade recession gets worse or better depends very much on whether people expect it to get worse or better. Even the efficacy of some steps which may be taken to reverse it, such as a reduction of taxation, depends to an important extent on whether people expect them to succeed.

Implicit and unconscious assumptions are no less basic to the internal relations on which the stability of a system usually depends. The division of labour, within an organization, no less than between it and others, depends on a network of mutual expectations, of which the most important are unconscious.

Let me at this point distinguish between three related ideas, expectation, confidence and co-operation. By expectation I mean simply the power to make representations of the future, itself a derivative of our power to represent the hypothetical. It does not imply any particular degree of certainty; and the idea of certainty is itself a little uncertain. At a roulette table I am certain that the result will be dictated by chance and this certainty, whilst it rules out short-term prediction, enables me to make some long-term ones with a high degree of precision.

Most business decisions involve attaching degrees of probability to various hypotheses; and with refinements in mathematical and electronic techniques we may become able to handle probabilities in the future with much greater precision. Expectation does not imply certainty.

But for purposes of action it is useful to be able to attach to some expectations such a degree of assurance that we can act on the assumption that they will occur. I think it convenient to keep the word 'confidence' for our attitude towards expectations of this kind, expectations which, though they are hypothetical, do not require us to apply probability factors or to work out alternatives on the supposition that they will not be realized.

Unhappily, the word 'confidence', when applied to the mutual relations of men, has acquired an overtone, linking it to co-operation. I want to exclude this overtone from our discussion. I am confident that my business colleague will do all he can to make my work easy and effective; but I am equally confident that my competitor will try to outsell me. In war I am confident that my enemy will destroy me if he can. And all three confidences are guides to action, giving me far more guidance than I should have, if I did not know whether my opposite number was friend, competitor or enemy. I regard co-operation, competition and conflict as three distinct and characteristic forms of human interaction; and expectation, including those assured expectations in which we can feel confidence, regulates all three forms, though in co-operation they have greater extension and refinement for reasons which I mention later.

Expectations arise through experience but we must accord a special place to that peculiar kind of human experience which consists in receiving verbal communications. Thus I may go to market in the expectation that I shall be able to buy some tomatoes, merely because in the past I have always found them there. But equally my expectations may derive from the fact that I have ordered them and that the merchant promised to have some. At first sight it would seem that a single promise has cut out the need for a long process of experience but this, of course, is not so. My confidence in the promise reflects a long experience of promises; and not merely of promises but of promises being kept. The information conveyed by language depends not merely on the semantic capacity of the language but on the confidence with which it is received. Thus communication both depends on and contributes to those structures of expectation on which economic systems, like other human systems, depend so much for the regulation of their inner and outer relations.

The deliberate building and moulding of these structures of expectation form a large part of business activity. Externally, the goodwill of a business is the sum of the expectations entertained in regard to it by customers, suppliers, employees, investors and the general public. Advertising is directed to building up in the minds of potential customers expectations which clamour to be satisfied. In the field of internal relations the building of stable systems of expectation is a growing activity of management. An organization is a structure of roles, to which functions are attached. If these are known and are suitably related to each other, the organization will remain coherent and effective, though men come and go; for newcomers will find themselves guided and supported by the structure of expectations which has become attached to their roles, defining what the holder can expect of others and what they expect of him; and each will act on the basis of these expectations, unless and until they are destroyed by further experience. This stability is a pre-condition of effective, collective action over long spans of time.

It also imports what may be a dangerous rigidity. Any change in organization which re-distributes roles, and especially one which splits the functions previously associated with one role is likely to create confusion proportionate to the degree to which the previous structure of expectations was well established. Much attention has lately been given to the problem of minimizing such disturbances. Everyone knows from experience that it is not enough to issue a new directive, however clear; and much has been learned about the conditions in which men will adapt themselves most quickly to such changes.

One of these is the presence of confidence in that special sense to which I referred earlier. This has two constituents. It includes the assurance that the other will perform the functions which attach to his role competently, including those discretionary functions which are its most important element. It includes also the negative assurance that the other will not use his position in a way inconsistent with another set of expectations, the set which define the ethics of the situation – that, for example, he will not use his position to pay off private scores or to steal credit for other people's work or to do any of the other things which in the particular circumstances of time and place he is expected not to do.

The reason why confidence in this sense is so important to co-operation is that in any large organization people are constantly being embarrassed by the decisions of their colleagues and seldom have the opportunity to form their own view whether the decision was right. They have to take nearly everything on trust. I happen to have served in two organizations which sprang into existence from a blueprint, rather than by a natural process of growth and in which consequently these assumptions were at first weak or lacking, so I have had occasion to observe how utterly this condition limits what can be done and increases the strain of doing what little is possible.

There is an inherent difference between the growth of mutual expectations between men and the growth of other expectations. Since, when men are in interaction, each is able to build hypothetical models not merely of his own expectations of the other but also of the other's expectations in regard to him and to his still hypothetical behaviour, there arises possibilities of understanding and of misunderstanding, of co-operation and of deceit, such as is not otherwise possible. Vicious circles and gracious circles, those ubiquitous phenomena, attain their most extreme elaboration in human relations; and they do so through the human capacity for expectation.

I have been talking about one of the governors of human behaviour, part of our familiar control mechanisms, which we know not only from introspection but from observation. So far as I know, we lack at present a conceptual model adequate to relate these controls, which I have described at the business level, to the rest of our knowledge about human and non-human behaviour. Psychologists could greatly help economists and business men by providing such a model. Hitherto they may have been deterred by the teleological overtones which attach to such words as 'intention' and 'expectation'. Today I hope the enterprise may be attempted without hazard to scientific respectability, since we are developing a language apt to describe the self-control of open systems of all kinds. I will venture some suggestions for filling this gap or at least for defining more clearly the gap to be filled.

First, we need a better model of the cognitive process by which the brain abstracts regularities from the stream of experience and uses these abstractions to classify future experience, a circular process which progressively determines what further experience it can assimilate and in what form. Creatures much simpler than we structure their perceptual experience in this way, by comparing abstracted features with pre-existing patterns, innate or learned. The process involves matching and it is of some complexity, even in its simplest form. The herring gull chick responds not directly to the red patch on the feeding bill but to the similarity between an observed red patch, itself an abstraction, and a pattern which has been built in; a similarity not absolute but falling within limits of tolerance which are themselves built in.

Learned cues may be far more elaborate; they may include patterns in time as well as space and can thus represent change with time – how else could swifts feed on the wing?

Clearly the cognitive capacity of the brain in man has been notably developed. We can classify experience in a greater variety of overlapping categories. We can build hypothetical representations of experience as it is and as it might be, both on a time base; and we can include therein representations of our hypothetical selves. This has vastly extended the controls which we can derive from comparing the two sets of representation. But the basic faculty or at least the basic principle seems common to nervous systems much simpler than our own. All cognition is re-cognition.

I suggest that the processes by which business controls its operations through the explicit building and projection of estimates and standards parallel and illuminate the less conscious processes of the individual mind. I have little doubt that a clearer model of this process would help to make more precise the mechanisms of adaptation at the human level and the ways in which these mechanisms break down.

Consider two familiar ways. A long-term and ambitious policy requires us to live for a long time with a stream of imperious mis-match signals which no immediate action can abate. The disparity between the 'is' and the 'ought to be' is sharp and can be corrected only over years. The tension is correspondingly great and is none the less for the fact that the disparity has been created by the policy decision.

Again, a well-balanced policy requires us to live with many streams of mis-match signals, prompting us to inconsistent action. Short-term profit, long-term stability, internal coherence, public relations – all these are names for standards with which the obdurate course of events has to be brought into line. Stress in the boardroom may be well defined in terms of the number, the loudness and the inconsistency of the streams of mis-match signals which fight for attention. It may be that the concept of stress in the individual mind might be made somewhat less imprecise by the use of the same conceptual model.

For any survey of the role of expectation in business must point the fact that expectation multiplies and makes explicit the awareness of conflict; and this is its most useful, as well as its most painful feature. Every action is a link not merely in the sequence of action in which it arises but in many others also; and in some of these other contexts it is bound to be unwelcome. For A the proposed development of a housing estate is a way to get people housed. For B it is an addition to the rateable value of the area and to the demands on the rates. For C it is a threat to a Green Belt; for D an increase in traffic load on a road; for E an attempt by F at empire building; for G a threat to the coherence of his administrative team. All these disparates are relevant; but how are they weighed against each other? Or is weighing an inept analogy?

There is here, I suggest, a further gap to be filled in the conceptual model. For it is clear that such decisions involve both weighing and matching and that the two are separate but related. If, as I am suggesting, our responses are linked to the way we classify the situation, they will be determined cognitively, by matching rather than by weighing; but the classification will be affected by anticipation of the action to which it will lead. Most revaluations are only re-classifications. I once participated, as a lawyer, in a decision which took fourteen months of agonized and tedious debate. These were made tolerable for me by watching the one board member who realized in the first five minutes that one solution was bound to triumph in the end, if only decision could be deferred until his colleagues had brought themselves to revise their initial classification of the situation, so as to admit of an adaptive response. The reappraisal, when it came, was a cognitive act, a decision to regard the situation as being primarily of type A rather than type B – it being clearly both; but this decision would not have been made but for its dynamic implications.

In this paper I have used the word 'control' in a sense much wider than 'keeping constant'. Deviation from a norm or approach to a limit may be used to signal the need for corrective action, whether the standard so used is constant or not. Often in business the standard set is a constantly expanding one; it may none the less prove an effective governor.

The language which I have been using is still associated too closely with the idea of homeostasis. True, the homeostatic devices with which physiology has made us familiar, such as temperature control, hold constant the *'milieu interieur'*; but at the same time the body as a whole is conforming in an equally controlled way to the expanding pattern of growth and maturation. Homeostasis is only a special case of control, within a context of much wider scope. Professor Waddington[1] has suggested the word 'homeorhesis' to fill this linguistic gap.

Our biological governors are built in, though even these can achieve more complex patterns than holding constant. Our psychological governors are more plastic; they pursue an unpredictable course of change and development within the experience of a single lifetime.

In the setting of these positive and negative governors, far more than in the devising of new responses, lies the scope for human adaptation. When we better understand how these governors are set, we may find that some of the processes which are made conscious and explicit in the control of business are closely analogous to the workings of the individual mind.

REFERENCE

[1] Waddington, C. H., *The Strategy of the Gene*. (1957) London: Allen and Unwin.

CHAPTER FOUR

Judgment*

I AM HONOURED to have been asked to give the sixth in this series of lectures, founded to perpetuate the memory of Edward Tregaskiss Elbourne, to whom, as founder of the Institute of Industrial Administration, the British Institute of Management owes a special, as well as a general, debt of gratitude. My five predecessors have painted comprehensive pictures, worthy of the wide-ranging interests and unifying concepts of the man we are here to honour. My approach is more selective. I ask you to consider only one of the qualities which are needed for management: the quality of good judgment. But my short title will invite us to a longer journey than we shall compass in the period of the lecture.

I choose this subject because it fascinates me, but I have more respectable reasons for my choice. Judgment is an important quality in a manager; perhaps more eagerly sought and more highly paid than any. It is also an elusive quality, easier to recognize than to define, easier to define than to teach. To some it has an aura of mystery, suggesting unidentified, intuitive powers behind the inexplicably accurate hunch. Others believe that its deepest secrets are already familiar to those who programme computers. Our language and our thought on the subject are alike, imprecise. If I can contribute to their better ordering, I feel that I shall be doing something worthy, at least in intention, of an Elbourne lecturer.

We use the word 'judgment' in many contexts. Applying it to business executives, we have in mind, I think, the power of reaching 'right' decisions (whatever that may mean) when the apparent criteria are so

*The sixth Elbourne Memorial Lecture – given to the British Institute of Management, November 1960.

complex, inadequate, doubtful or conflicting as to defeat the ordinary
man. Even in this sense judgment is, of course, not confined to business
executives for it is required equally by statesmen, generals and princes
of the Church; and even in this sense we may be unsure where it begins
and ends. When our Government in 1940 shipped tanks to Egypt,
through precarious seas, away from a country still in danger, to take
part in operations still unplanned, Sir Winston Churchill took responsibility for a decision, apparently rash, which was justified by results.
Shall we call this 'good judgment'? What of the decision of Bolivar,
when, in the swampy delta of the Orinoco, he announced to a few ragged
followers that he had that day founded the Republic of Gran Columbia
and had fixed its capital at Bogota, a thousand miles away across the
Andes? He too was justified by results. Are these exercises of the same
faculty which led Mr Henry Ford to create Model T40?

Judges of the Supreme Court exercise judgment; yet politicians and
civil servants, who take what they call administrative decisions, have
generally maintained, in a controversy now thirty years old, that the
rightness of their judgments is not a matter which courts of law can
competently review. The opposite view is now gaining ground. What
is the difference between the judgment of judges and the judgment of
administrators?

What of the scientists? Vesalius rejected the view, accepted in his
day, that the dividing wall of the heart is pierced by invisible passages.
He proved to be right, and he is rightly remembered as a hero of scientific scepticism. Harvey assumed the existence of invisible passages con-
necting the arteries with the veins, an assumption then new and commended only by the fact that it was required by his theory of the
circulation of the blood. He proved to be right too; and he is rightly
remembered as a hero of – scientific intuition. Did these two men show
'good judgment' in the same sense?

What of the doctor making a diagnosis? What of the artist painting
out a tone or a form which, in his judgment, disturbs the balance of his
picture? What of the connoisseur who chooses that artist's work from
among a hundred others, because he judges it to be of higher and more
enduring merit? What of the man in a moral dilemma who judges one

personal claim on him to be more weighty than another; and of his neighbours, who judge his decision as right or wrong? All these are exercising judgment; and though their fields are remote from that of the business executive, their activities are not. For the business executive also has occasion to act judicially, to make diagnoses, to weigh moral issues, to judge as connoisseur, even, perhaps, to compose in his own medium as an artist. It seems that we shall have to decide whether the word 'judgment' in all these contexts stand for one mental activity or many

I shall distinguish three broad types of judgment. Harvey and Vesalius made judgments about the state of affairs 'out there'. They revised the currently accepted view of external reality. I will call such judgments 'reality judgments'.

Churchill, Bolivar and Ford also made reality judgments; but they went further. They made judgments of what to do about it; and they committed themselves to action on the basis of these judgments. I will call such judgments 'action judgments'. In my examples, what strikes us most about their action judgment is that it 'came off'. In each case it achieved the desired result.

There is, however, a third element in these judgments – the judgment of what result was most to be desired. This I will call a value judgment. Churchill, Bolivar and Ford would not be remembered in these contexts unless they had been convinced of the value of victory in the Middle East, of creating independent republics of the Spanish-American colonies, of building a popular car; and these were not the only judgments of value which underlay their decisions.

In each case the value judgment is separate from the action judgment; it can be separately criticized. That the action succeeded does not prove that it was well conceived. Some strategists criticized the British emphasis on the Middle Eastern theatre of war. San Martin thought that the new states of South America should have been set up as a constitutional monarchies. Even Henry Ford's 'tin Lizzie' was criticized – on aesthetic grounds. Hindsight often leads us to wish that our well-laid plans had failed.

I shall return in a moment to consider the part played by these three kinds of judgment – value judgment, reality judgment, action judgment – in the making of business decisions. First, I want to inquire how we recognize these judgments as good. The answer is curious and somewhat disturbing.

The capillaries which were invisible to Harvey can now be demonstrated by improved microscopy. His judgment has been confirmed by observation. Yet even the so-called facts of observation need judgment to give them meaning, a judgment often difficult and hazardous. Moreover, few reality judgments can be confirmed by observation, even after the event; for many relevant facts of a situation – the state of someone's mind, for example – are not observable and change constantly and unpredictably, not least through the effects of judgments made about them. In the ultimate analysis, all reality judgments are matters of inference and can be confirmed or challenged only be new reality judgments, based on further inferences.

With action judgments we feel on firmer ground; we can check them against their results. Yet this is at best a rough and ready test, especially at the level of my examples. Who can say whether the courses which were not tried would not have worked out better than the one which was chosen? Moreover, every choice involves weighing probabilities. The course rightly chosen as of least risk may none the less prove lethal; the course of most risk may still come off. Results no doubt confirm judgments with some assurance when similar choices are repeated in controlled conditions often enough for the laws of probability to speak with authority; but it is hard to see how such an objective test can be applied to the judgments of the statesman or the top executive. It would seem that the validation of action judgments also is a matter of judgment.

When we consider value judgments we find the same situation in a much more extreme form. The validation of a value judgment is necessarily a value judgment. Churchill, Bolivar and Ford told themselves

48

what they meant by success. Those who disagreed with them could do so only by appealing to different standards, representing value judgments of their own. There would seem to be no means whereby the adjudicating mind can escape responsibility for the standards of value to which it commits itself.

I have distinguished three kinds of judgment, often present together – value judgment, reality judgment and action judgment – and I have reached the conclusion that the higher the level of judgment involved, the less possible it is to find an objective test by which to prove that the judgment is good. The appraisal of judgment is itself an act of judgment. In particular, value judgments are logically incapable of being validated by any objective test. They cannot be proved true or false. They can only be approved as right or condemned as wrong by the exercise of another value judgment.

Does this condemn us to pure subjectivism? In my view definitely not. The status of judgments which are neither objective nor subjective has been analysed on a grand scale, with special regard to scientific judgments, by Professor Michael Polanyi,[1] himself an outstanding physical scientist – and I find myself broadly in agreement with his views, as far as I understand them – but to pursue the philosophic issue involved would take me far beyond the limits of this lecture. Nor need I do so, for the concept of responsible choice – that is, of decision which is personal yet made with a sense of obligation to discover the 'rules of rightness'[2] applicable to the particular situation – is a familiar concept in business, which we trust and use many times a day, even though neither philosophers nor psychologists can explain it.

We sometimes use the word 'judgment' as if it meant the same as 'decision', but this is too narrow an interpretation. A good judge of men, for example, *reveals* his good judgment by the appointments and changes he makes, but the judgment which guides those decisions is something which he exercises continually as he observes and appraises the people around him. I will ask you to consider an example of this sort in some detail.

One morning, Mr Redletter, the managing director of The Weather-cock Company (all the characters in my illustrations are imaginary) reached the conclusion that the company's chief supplies officer, Mr A, was not up to his job; that somehow he must be removed from his post and replaced by Mr B. What precipitated this decision I will inquire later. For the moment I ask you to accept it as a fact and to follow it backwards and forwards in time.

To reach this conclusion Mr Redletter must have had in his head an idea of where the Weathercock Company was going and of where it wanted it to go; of the part which the supplies department was playing in the comapny's effectiveness and the part which it should be playing; of Mr A's performance as its head and of what its head's performance should be; and of the probable performance of Mr B. All these ideas were the cumulative result of several years' experience of the company and its staff. They were not mere observations, they were judgments. These judgments go in pairs; a judgment of the situation as it is, is compared with a judgment of the situation as it might be. It is the disparity between the two which has moved Mr Redletter to his decision. These are the two types of judgment which I have already distinguished as reality judgment and value judgment. They are closely connected.

Mr Redletters' idea of Mr A is not a mere catalogue of Mr A's past performances. It is an hypothesis sufficiently comprehensive to explain all he knows about Mr A, and from which he can assess Mr A's probable performance in various roles; his potentialities and power of learning; his current trend of development or deterioriation; his probable response to promotion or transfer. Even so, it is not complete. It is selective and the selection reflects the nature of his interest in Mr A, which is that of a manager in a functional subordinate. Mr A's doctor or wife or colleague on the local borough council would each have a different picture of Mr A – different not merely because of their differing gifts and opportunities for forming a judgment, but also because of their differing interests in Mr A. Someone who had no interest in Mr A could have no picture of him at all.

Thus the nature of Mr Redletter's interest in Mr A defines what aspects of Mr A he shall select for attention and valuation. The same is true of his interest in the supplies department. So when Mr Redletter asked himself, 'Can we wear Mr A any longer as Chief Supplies Officer?', he found the materials for an answer already in his head. Nor were these merely 'raw' materials. They were an accumulation of judgments, leading to ever more complete hypotheses about Mr A and the supplies department. On the other hand, what he found in his head was not *the* answer. This question redefined his interest and called for a revaluation of the problem, leaving his ideas of Mr A and the supplies department however slightly changed.

The result we know. For the first time, on this particular morning, Mr Redletter, comparing his value judgment with his reality judgment, reached the answer 'no'.

Let us now follow that silent decision forwards. What is to be done? This I have called the action judgment. It takes the form of a dialogue between Mr Redletter, the man of judgment, and an invaluable but irritating boffin in his head who makes uncritical but sometimes brilliant suggestions.

'*Move him to another job?*'
　'He'd be worse elsewhere.'
'*Retire him early under the pension scheme?*'
　'We can't – he's below the minimum age.'
'*Give him his notice and let him go?*'
　'We couldn't do that with old A in all the circumstances, it wouldn't be fair.'
'*Make him an* ex gratia *allowance?*'
　'Anything big enough to mitigate hardship would be a most awkward precedent.'
'*Must you really do it now?*'
　'YES!'

　　　Silence: then –

'*Well, you could divide the department, leave A in charge of the bit he knows, put B in charge of the rest, let them both report to C for the time being; then, in two years when C retires . . .*'
　'M' yes. We *might . . .*'

You will notice that all these tentative action judgments except the last one are rejected because they are either impracticable or inconsistent with Mr Redletter's idea of the sort of employer the company wished to be: in other words, by a reality judgment or a value judgment.

I have now squeezed all I want from this example. I summarize the results.

(1) Judgment is a fundamental, continuous process, integral with our thinking.

(2) It has three aspects – for simplicity, three kinds of judgment – value judgment, reality judgment, action judgment. The first two are the more fundamental and important. Action judgment is only called for by the interaction of value judgment and reality judgment, and is only selected by further use of the same criteria.

(3) The aspects of the situation which are appreciated (reality judgment) and evaluated (value judgment) are determined by the interest of the judging mind.

All these forms of judgment are mental skills. It remains to ask in what they consist, e.g. and how they may be trained. Before I turn to these questions I will take up one which I have left unanswered. Why did Mr Redletter reach his conclusion just then? This inquiry will lead me to explore the meaning of initiative and the relation between initiative and judgment.

What precipitated Mr Redletter's action judgment? Had Mr A just dropped an enormous 'clanger', costing the company most of a year's profit? Or had Mr Redletter so radically revised his ideas of what a supplies department should be that Mr A's interpretation of his role, though unchanged and accepted for many years, suddenly became intolerable?

These are remote points on a continuous scale. The disparity between reality judgment and value judgment may widen because of a change either in the situation as we see it (our reality judgment) or in the standards of value which we apply to it (our value judgment). This scale is important and I will illustrate it by two other episodes in the earlier history of the Weathercock Company. The decision involved in both is collective. What I have said applies equally, as I believe, to collective and to individual decisions. In collective decisions, however, varying views on reality, value and action are expressed by different voices and are more easily distinguished than when their clashes and accommodations take place within a single head.

The first episode presents the directors of the Weathercock Company in an emergency meeting one Thursday. The bank has refused to extend the overdraft sufficiently to provide the pay packets on the following day except upon unwelcome and onerous terms. After long debate, the directors accept the bank's terms, telling each other that they have no choice. Strictly speaking they had a choice; they might have said 'no' or failed to say 'yes', which would have been the same thing. To choose this alternative, however, would be to choose the immediate and irreversible dissolution of the undertaking and of their own authority, and that in the most untidy fashion. The bank's terms raised no objections which could make such a course preferable.

I will now introduce you to the board of the Weathercock Company some years later. The situation has been transformed. Output is maximal, orders and cash are alike embarrassing in their abundance. The only troubles are troubles of growth, and the worst of these is that the company has no longer any physical room to grow.

They are agreed that something must be done but embarrassed by the variety of possible courses and divided on the merits of the few which are seriously considered. Mr. Redletter wants to build a new factory on a new site in a new town twenty miles away; and in it he wants an impressive slice of space to develop a new business in moulded plastics, which, with the reluctant consent of his board, he had set up in some precious floor space of the present works a year or two before.

None of his colleagues supports the managing director; the arguments against his plan are impressive. The firm will lose most of its present employees and face others with hard choices. It will break its connections with its home town and its home site. The economies claimed for the move are offset by an x representing the unknown variables which will be set loose by so radical a change. And why moulded plastics, when the traditional business is doing so well?

The final decision was in no one's mind when the debate began but was unanimously adopted in the end and pleased everyone. The under-taking would stay where it was, make better use of existing space, and would swallow the coveted area begrudged to plastics. It would also buy a large site in the place favoured by Mr Redletter and build there a small factory – for the moulded plastic business only. Mr Redletter was well content. His pet venture could expand all the better in this relative isolation; the rest could still move out, maybe, one day later on. The others were content also. They got what they wanted, escaped all threats – and kept the managing director happy. You will note that the managing director, though in a minority of one, got his way in what most mattered to him, because all his colleagues felt it was essential to any settlement that they should keep him, and keep him happy. These two situations illustrate what I will call the gradient of initiative.

The first is an extreme case. The company is on the verge of insolvency. An instability – the imbalance between money in and money out – which has been progressively affecting its performance for some time, is about to cross a critical threshold, beyond which its effects will over-flow in all directions and bring the system to disorganization and dis-solution.

The effect of instability on a system is usually of this form. The most clear-cut example is physical death. A living organism is an organiza-tion, maintained by the delicately balanced intake and outflow of air, food and water, and equipped with admirable devices for keeping these balances – and many others – within critical limits. The maintenance of this system is a necessary, though not of course a sufficient, condition for the highest achievement of human intellect and feeling; and among the humble but necessary skills of living we recognize the skill of keep-ing alive and healthy – normally as a condition of all we want to do with life, occasionally, as when we are escaping from a fire or a furious bull, as an end in itself.

Similarly, for businesses, solvency is not an end, but it is a pre-condi-tion of successful existence and when threatened it may become an end in itself.

Political organizations such as nation states are similarly liable to changes of this step-function form. There is, however, a difference in the degree of irreversible change illustrated by these examples. The dead organism dissolves; all its constituents rearrange themselves in new and less improbable configurations. The bankrupt business, after liquidation, may reappear more or less changed. Someone will probably carry on much the same business in the same building with some of the old plant. Some of the former employees may be re-engaged. Only the accounts will show a complete break. Alternatively, if technical liquidation is avoided, the only continuity may be the old losses, carefully preserved for the benefit of the newcomer's future income tax.

Wars and political revolutions raise even more difficult questions as to the identity of the future system with that of the past. These difficulties are due largely to our habits of language and thought, which invest their objects with an unreal degree of wholeness and independence. I refer to them only to establish two ideas which are important to my argument.

I wish to distinguish first between the conditions which establish a given measure of freedom and the reasons which explain how that freedom is actually used. In my case-history, the establishment of the company's liquidity was one of the conditions which enabled it to grow and ultimately to go in for moulding plastics; but it throws no light at all on why the company chose to go in for moulding plastics. For this we must explore the past history of the managing director.

This may seem obvious; but it is often by no means easy to be sure whether a given explanation explains why something happened or merely explains how its happening was possible. The theory of evolution has been supposed for the last century to explain why life on this planet has developed as it has; but serious and respected thinkers today contend that the theory merely explains how that development, among others, became possible.[3]

Arising out of this distinction, I wish to establish the idea that an organization, like an organism, can conveniently be regarded as a hierarchy of systems, each dependent on, but not explained by, those below. The variables which determine the solvency of a business could be described and discussed without any reference to the nature of the under-taking's product, the interests of its staff, the ambitions of its directors or a host of other things which fill the agenda at its meetings. In the first situation, solvency was in such peril that the field of choice was minimal. As with the man escaping from the bull, the preservation of basic conditions had become itself a dominating goal of policy. In the second situation, the basic conditions of existence were sufficiently se-cure to enable the directors to realize a variety of possible values, even some which they had not contemplated before. The future depended not on the adroitness of their actions but on the quality of their dreams. The gradient of initiative leads from the familiar track, where events are in control, to the uncharted spaces where dreams, whether 'right' dreams or 'wrong' dreams, can and must take charge and where that man is lost who cannot dream at all.

Thus skill in value judgment is increasingly demanded as human initiative widens. It is to be expected that some leaders who show the greatest resource in conditions of extreme difficulty will be less success-ful when they must seek guidance, not from without, but from within themselves.

I will now revert to the question left unanswered at the end of an ear-lier section. What are the mental processes underlying the three aspects of judgment?

The judgment which has been most carefully studied is what I have called the 'pure' action judgment. This is typified in Köhler's classic learning experiments with apes. The motivation (value judgment) is standardized; the animal wants a bunch of bananas which is out of reach. The situation is standardized; the materials for a solution are all in sight. Only one solution is possible, so no choice between solutions is involved. The means to be used – a hooked stock, a few boxes – are not, as far as can be avoided, charged with an affective meaning of their own. The issue is simply whether the creature can see how to use these neutral objects as means to an end.

The process by which one ape does, while another ape does not, succeed – suddenly, but after prolonged incubation – in 'seeing' the boxes as a potential increase in height, the stick as a potential increase in reach, remains a fascinating psychological puzzle.

Now consider a human example. As a very inexperienced subaltern in the old war, my company commander once said to me, 'Vickers, the company will bathe this afternoon. Arrange.' In the Flemish hamlet where we were billeted the only bath of any kind was in the local nunnery. The nuns were charity itself but I could not ask them to bathe a hundred men. I reviewed other fluid-containing objects – cattle drinking troughs, empty beer barrels – and found practical or ethical objections to them all; and at that point I had the misfortune to meet my company commander again and was forced to admit that I had not yet found the answer. He was annoyed. 'Whatever have you been doing all this time?' he said, and then, turning his own mind to the problem, as it seemed for the first time, he added, 'Take the company limbers off their wheels, put the tilts inside, four baths each four feet square, four men to a bath, do the job in an hour, why don't you use your brains?'

Simple indeed; but his solution involved two steps which my mind had not taken – the apprehension that a vehicle is a collection of bits and pieces, of which, for some purposes, the wheels may be irrelevant: and the apprehension that a tilt tailored to cover a protruding load and keep rain-water out, would fit and serve equally well, pushed into the empty waggon, to keep bath-water in.

My company commander – unlike myself – showed a mental ability like that of Köhler's more successful apes, though higher in degree; a facility for uncoupling the elements of a familiar idea and recombining them in a new way – for seeing a limber as two potential baths on irrelevant wheels, without forgetting that it is primarily and must again become a vehicle. This is a faculty useful in the research and development department and equally in the board-room. Let us call it ingenuity.

Yet it must involve more than we usually associate with ingenuity. The mere multiplication of alternative means to an end might only make the choice harder, unless it were accompanied by some gift which guides the problem-solver in the general direction of the still undiscovered solution. The literature of problem solving, no less than common experience, attests our capacity for searching with a lively sense of 'warm ... warmer ... *warmer* ...', when we do not know what we are looking for.

It would seem then that even the pure action judgment involves mental faculties which are still highly obscure. Yet the pure action judgment is too simple a process to be seen outside the laboratory. Even my efforts to improvise bathing facilities were hedged about with reality judgments and value judgments of great complexity; reality judgments about what our Flemish hosts would stand with equanimity from their British billetees, and value judgments defining the kind of solution which would be acceptable to me, having regard to its impact on the troops, the inhabitants, my company commander and myself.

The action judgment is involved in answering any question of the form, 'What shall I do about it?' when 'it' has been defined by judgments of reality and value. In implementing a decision, this question may have to be asked several times. 'What shall we do about the supplies department?' 'We will change the head.' 'What shall we do about changing the head?' 'We will divide the department and ...' 'What shall we do about this decision to divide ... ?' 'First we will tell A and then B and then ...'

Thus each decision sets a more precise problem for the next exercise of action judgment; and at each stage there is assumed a set of criteria for determining between different solutions. These criteria are supplied by further judgments of reality and value. 'That would not be legal.' 'That would not be fair.' 'That would not be possible.' And so on.

This process has many interesting aspects which I have no time to pursue. I will refer to two only.

First, what solutions are considered and in what order? Professor Simon[4] has pointed out that the solutions which are weighed are usually far fewer than the totality of possible solutions which exist. Often the totality is too large to be reviewed, however briefly, in the time available. Random selection seldom if ever occurs. Some mental process narrows the field rapidly to a short list of alternatives, which alone are carefully compared.

Some elements of this selective process are apparent. A man seeking a solution to a problem will usually review first the solutions which are approved by custom or his own experience for dealing with problems which seem similar; or he may try first the responses which are most accessible to him or which he most enjoys. Occasionally, however, explanations fail us and we have to credit the problem-solver with an intuitive feeling for the approach which is likely to prove fruitful, though we can see no clue by which it is recognized. This is the heuristic element in ingenuity, to which I have already referred.

It is sometimes assumed that the fully rational course is to examine every possible solution and to choose the 'best'. It seems clear to me that this is not the way the brain works. The criterion, I suggest, is not the best but the 'good enough'. The human brain scans possible solutions in an order which is itself determined by the complex and obscure factors to which I have referred; and it stops as soon as a solution is not rejected by criteria of reality or value.

If all solutions are rejected and no new ones can be devised, the standard of the acceptable has to be lowered and the process is then repeated. The unsuccessful series of rehearsals is not wasted, for it prepares the mind for the change of standard.

I turn now to the reality judgment. This, too, involves analysis and synthesis, often repeated. It requires the ready handling, dissociating, reassociating of the elements in our thought which I have called ideas or concepts. It, too, has scope for ingenuity. Yet it seems to me to require somewhat different qualities of mind.

The problem-solver has his problem to guide him. The reality judgment, on the other hand, leads us as far afield as we let it; for the aspect of the situation with which it is concerned is as wide as our interest, and we can follow it in time until imagination fails us. One of the gifts needed by those who make reality judgments is to know where to stop: to sense the point beyond which the best estimate of trends is not worth making.

The maker of reality judgments is for the time being an observer; not like the maker of action judgments, an agent. He needs detachment, objectivity, balance, a clear head to follow the complex permutations of the possible and the practicable; a stout heart, to give as much reality to the unwelcome as to the welcome. Where the maker of action judgments must above all be ingenious, persistent, and bold, the maker of reality judgments must be honest, clear-sighted and brave. Above all, perhaps, he needs a ready sense for those aspects of the situation which are most relevant. And here, too, the man of outstanding judgment shows such an unerring sense for those facts which will be found to matter most that it is safer to give his unexplained facility a special name and call it also an heuristic gift.

The value judgment raises problems far more obscure. Clearly it is fundamental; if we were not concerned with values which we wanted to realize and preserve, we should have no interest in the situation and no incentive to action. The basic difficulty in all complex decisions is to reconcile the conflicting values involved – in my first example, the supply needs of the undertaking, the deserts of Mr A, the board's reputation as an employer, the preservation of tacit rules governing promotion and discharge and so on.

All these values are standards of what the undertaking should seek and expect of itself and others. I will call them norms. They are not stated in abstract terms but they are implicit in every major decision. Executives absorb them from these decisions and still more from the experience of participating in the making of decisions, and by the same process they contribute to the setting of these standards and to their constant revision. Thus the maker of value judgments is not an observer but an agent. He needs not so much detachment as commitment, for his judgment commits him to implications far wider than he can know.

In approaching their decisions, executives usually find the appropriate standards of value ready to hand. They cannot depart aburptly either from their own past standard or from those current in their industry. In deciding how to treat Mr A, for example, the possible range of decision was closely limited. Thus executives, in making value judgments, are seldom conscious of doing more than apply a rule.

Yet, viewed over time, it is obvious that these standards are constantly changed by the very process of applying them, just as the common law is developed and changed by accumulating precedents. The ghost of the economic man should not persuade us to ignore the fact that business undertakings today are governed by most complex value systems. Those who direct them must somehow provide themselves with standards of what the undertaking expects of itself – standards sufficiently coherent to be usable, yet sufficiently comprehensive to define its divergent responsibilities to employees, shareholders, consumers, suppliers, locality, industry, government and community. In every one of these fields the standards of industry today are markedly different from what they were a few decades ago; and the standards of individual undertakings differ from one to another and also change with time.

Thus in every value judgment there is latent a creative process; a resetting of the norms which are being applied.

We can as yet give no satisfactory account of the process by which we resolve problems of conflicting value. We only beg the question when we talk of maximizing satisfactions, for the satisfactions we maximize are set by ourselves; and there is no evidence that we reduce those disparate imponderables to a common measure, so that they can be added and weighed. There is indeed much evidence that we do not.

I have already expressed the belief that in the ultimate analysis, the validity of our norm-setting cannot be validated or falsified by results. It can be approved or condemned only be reference to a sense of rightness for which the adjudicating mind must take responsibility. This is obviously true of the artist and the connoisseur of art and conduct. That it is equally true of the scientist is the theme of Professor Polanyi's book. I believe it to be equally true of the business executive.

This survey of the processes involved in judgment may well leave us in doubt how far the mechanical and mathematical models of decision-making – now so popular – as distinct from mechanical and mathematical aids to decision-making are of any relevance. On this important and controversial question I have time for only one comment. In so far as these models are concerned only with what I have called pure action judgment they would seem to have no bearing on any of the main issues which I have raised; for the pure action judgment is unknown in real life. In so far as they assert or suggest that the pure action judgment is the typical decision-making situation, they do a vast disservice both to the inquiry and to the undoubtedly great contribution which, with a more modest approach, they could make to it.

The extent to which we can develop judgment in ourselves and others is limited by our, and their, inherent capacity for the many mental activities involved. In these it seems clear that human beings differ widely. Minds differ greatly in their capacity for handling, arranging and combining the symbols with which we think. They differ in their ability to recognize causal and other relationships within actual or imagined sequences of events. We can say with confidence of some problems that they are too difficult for A to solve: of some situations that they are too complex for B to comprehend.

It may even be that men differ in the faculties they use. Dr Grey Walter[5] has suggested that those who are unusually gifted with visual imagination reach some decisions in ways quite different from the ways used by others, not less intelligent, who are unusually devoid of this gift. He claims further that the electro-encephalogram distinguishes the two types, each of which contains, he suggests, about a tenth of the population.

Men differ further in the moral qualities involved in judgment. C could comprehend the situation, he could solve the problem: but has he the guts to go on trying until he succeeds? Will the mere stress of having to try impair his capacity for success? (Examinations rightly test this moral quality, no less than the intellectual ones which they are designed to explore.) This difference is so important that we rate executives for decisiveness, as well as for good judgment, reserving the highest rewards for those who excel in both, but recognizing that the ability to decide at all is a prior requisite, and in some cases a major one. Lord Wavell, in some famous lectures on generalship, said that stupidity in generals should never excite surprise. For generals are chosen from that small, pre-selected class of men who are tough enough to be generals at all. From such heavy-duty animals, refinements of intellect and sensibility should not be expected.

Lord Wavell's dictum, to which he was so notable an exception, is of general application. No one can exercise good judgment unless he can support both the stress of the office in which the judgment is to be exercised, and the stress of the judgment itself. Not all high offices are in themselves as stressful as that of a general in the field; but the stress inherent in judgment itself is inescapable. Between value judgment and reality judgment there is tension, characteristic of all human life. It may lead to the kind of breakdown which psychiatrists meet in patients who have lost touch with reality, or who torment themselves with an impossible level of aspiration. Distortions of judgment due to the same cause are common enough in board-rooms, as for instance, when a board is faced with a problem of redundancy too large to be handled within the rules of what it has come to regard as fair. The opposite error of those who protect themselves by failing to aspire enough is more common, and much more wasteful, but more easily overlooked.

Again, the sheer difficulty of keeping the judgment of value and reality from running away into irresolvable complexity is itself a source of stress, and accounts for the familiar distinction between men of action and men of thought. The simplicity which characterizes the thought processes of men of action has often seemed to me excessive; but it is nevertheless essential to individual good judgment that a man's capacity for judgments of value and reality shall be related to his own capacity for action judgment. One of the merits of business organization is that these different human capacities can be combined by specializing functions.

Finally, clear judgment of value and reality only makes more frustrating the common human state of helplessness, when no effective action can be taken; and this is as common in business life as in life at large.

Courage and endurance are not the only moral qualities associated with good judgment. D has guts in plenty but he is conceited, full of personal prejudice, takes offence easily; in brief, is not sufficiently self-less or sufficiently disciplined to achieve that combination of detachment and commitment which good judgment demands.

Finally, apart from these moral qualities, I have expressed the belief that judgment needs that sensitivity to form, which, in various guises, distinguishes the connoisseur of art or conduct, the scientist and the judge, and which is equally required in the business executive.

Have I given the impression that good judgment is to be expected only from those who combine the qualities of philosopher, hero and saint to a degree rarely found even among top people? I hope not. In so far as it involves peculiarly human qualities of intellect, sensibility, character and will, it does indeed give scope for every kind of excellence, yet equally, just because it is so human a quality, it is not likely to be lacking in anyone we recognize as fully human.

It is indeed ubiquitous; for it is involved in some degree in every exercise of discretion. Among the debts of gratitude which business people owe to Dr Elliott Jaques, I give a high place to his finding[6] that, among all the jobs, from highest to lowest, in the undertaking which he has studied so carefully, there is some duty, essential to its performance, which is not and cannot be specified in the instructions given to the holder. We are not paid, says Dr Elliott Jaques, for doing what we are told to do, but for doing rightly that part of our job which is left to our discretion; and we rate our own and our fellows' jobs on our estimate of the weight of this discretionary element.

If Dr Elliott Jaques is right, judgment is the most universal requirement not only of managerial work but of all work. The distribution of roles on an organization chart may thus be seen, not merely as an allocation of duties but as an allocation of discretions, increasing up the hierarchy in the quality of the judgment they demand.

This picture helps us to answer the question, 'How is judgment developed?' The whole structure of industry is or should be a school of judgment, in the course of which individuals may develop, by practice and example, both the general qualities of mind, heart and will, which all judgment demands, and their own particular aptitudes which determine the kind of judgment in which they can become most proficient.

In such a school everyone is both learner and teacher. The teaching function is both positive and negative. It is positive in that it requires every member of the organization, in his daily work, to set an example in the exercise of judgment, and to supervise its exercise by those for whom he is responsible. It is negative in that it requires everyone to respect the field of discretion of his subordinates, as he expects his superiors to respect his own – especially when he himself is more expert than they in the very same field.

As I feared, my short title, like a conjuror's hat, has produced more curious objects than I have had time to examine to your satisfaction or my own. The material is far from tidy; the hat is far from empty; and my time is overspent. Apart from displaying what I believe to be the main dimensions of the problem and setting question marks in appropriate places, I have tried to do no more than to couple the higher executive – in the exercise of this, his most precious and highly-paid endowment – on the one hand, with those excellent minds in other fields, whose funtion he must so often copy unawares; on the other hand, to link him with the humblest servants in his own undertaking, on whose judgment he must rely, as they on his, and from among whom it should be his delight, as it is his duty, to develop minds capable of better judgment than his own.

REFERENCES

[1] Polanyi, M., *Personal Knowledge.* (1958) London: Routledge and Kegan Paul.

[2] The expression is Polanyi's. *op cit.*

[3] See, for example, Grene, M., *British Journal for Philosophy of Science.* (1958) Vol. ix, pp. 34 and 35.

[4] Simon, H. A., *Administrative Behaviour*. (2nd ed. 1959) New York: Macmillan.

[5] Walter D. W. Grey, *The Living Brain*. (1953) London: Duckworth, p. 152.

[6] Jaques, Elliott, *Measurement of Responsibility*. (1956) London: Tavistock Publications.

Criteria of Success

A SHARP distinction is sometimes drawn between business management and public administration. I believe that this distinction is much
less fundamental than is often supposed; that its importance is growing
less; and that it needs to diminish even further, if a mixed economy is
to be viable. I shall try to define the factors which are common to the
regulation of all kinds of organization and thus to determine what
difference, if any, there is in principle between the 'economic' decisions
of business and the 'political' decisions of government and public service.

I spent half my life as a corporation lawyer, designing organizations
to fit a multitude of different needs and conditions; and the other half,
as an administrator, helping to manage a variety of such undertakings.
The differences of which I was conscious as a lawyer had little relation
to the problems which concerned me as an administrator. Varied as
these were, their variety was much the same, whatever the nature of
the organization and whatever the object of its activities. Clearly there
is much in common in the management of, say, a government department, a public corporation, a private manufacturing enterprise, a law
firm, a professional body, a publicly administered hospital and a private
charity. What is it?

The most obvious common characteristic of all these organizations
is that they are all 'open systems' They maintain a form more enduring
than their constituents by constantly drawing from and returning to
the world around them materials, money and men. This is most obvious in a manufacturing industry as it converts raw materials into
finished products and scrap (consuming many other materials in the
process); but it is equally true of a newspaper or a city government or

a charity. The visible activity consists in streams of materials, money and men, flowing inwards and outwards at varying rates through invisible but enduring channels.

The proverb has it that we never step twice into the same river. It is equally true that we never go to work twice in the same undertaking. It is also equally false; for these words 'river' and 'undertaking' do not denote unchanging substances, but continuing forms. The language of business and administration is full of such words. Capital, revenue, profit and loss; stock, throughput, turnover, plant; staff, wastage, workload, capacity; all these and a hundred others refer to relations and aspects of relations between inflows and outflows, distinguished by administrators in the complex process which it is their job to regulate. Some of these words define the state of a balance at a point in time, like the balance in a bank account or the water level in a reservoir. Others define a rate of flow, such as the output from a production line or the volume of water over a dam, in some unit of time. Yet others define the relation between two rates of flow, as do profit and loss. All are descriptive of relationships.

There is nothing unusual in this. The familiar forms of language conceal from us the extent to which the objects of our attention are not 'things' but relations extended in time. I stress this, because the most essential common characteristic of the administrator's job in any organization is that he has to regulate a process extended in time.

The relations to which these words refer need not be constant; usually they are not. A bank balance is a bank balance, however much it fluctuates and whether it is black or red. It can even continue to exist at zero, so long as the account remains open. We have no difficulty in recognizing continuity through change, as well as time, provided the streams to which the relation refers continue to flow or are regarded as still capable of flowing.

On the other hand, organizations, like organisms and other open systems survive only so long as they keep their constituent variables within critical limits. Shortage of money, beyond a critical point, creates a self-exciting disturbance of relationships which overflows suddenly across all the activities of an undertaking, probably with irre-

versible effects; just as shortage of food, at a critical point, robs a creature of the energy to seek even the food it could get and starts a vicious
circle which involves the whole complex system in dissolution.

Organizations, unlike organisms, have usually no built-in programme to govern their future growth and it is not normally the task
of their regulators either to hold them constant or to follow a pre-
arranged development. But it is their task to keep the constituent flows
sufficiently in phase to enable the system to *survive*. Whether and how
far they are also permitted or expected to generate the resources for
future growth is a variable, marking one of the major distinctions[1]
between organizations of different types.

Thus the management of every organization involves what I will
call a balancing function of great complexity. A large number of inflows and outflows have to be kept at levels and within mutually related
limits which are necessary to survival. These are relations so like those
which enable an animal to go on generating the energy needed for
survival that I will call them metabolic relations.

These relations, however, can also be seen in another way. They
meet the needs of other systems; they thus serve a social function. They
would not long continue unless they continued to be valued by the
other parties to the relationship. Thus no organization – or so I shall
suggest – can be described in terms of balancing alone. It is concerned
also to fulfil the functions by which it lives; for these are conditions of
its continuance. Some of these are also among its own *purposes*, in that
their performance is regarded as a measure of success by the organization itself. Management is concerned to realize all these relations, in so
far as it can. Their demands are multiple and partly conflicting and
cannot all be fully realized with the resources available, so long as aspiration exceeds current possibilities of achievement – as our present
culture insists that it always should. So management, in addition to its
balancing function, has the task of realising what it judges to be the best
combination of these functions which it can achieve within the resources available to it; or at least a combination good enough to satisfy
its standards of success. It has thus what I will call an 'optimizing' function, though this would more exactly be called a 'satisficing' function,

to borrow a verb usefully coined by Professor Herbert Simon. I will refer to the combined administrative task as 'optimizing-balancing'.

The combination and the conflict of balancing and optimizing is best seen in an organization such as a local authority, which has multiple, specific responsibilities imposed on it by law. In each of its functional fields, education, health, welfare, housing, highways, police and so on, it is responsible for maintaining some relation or group of relations within the standards regarded as acceptable by itself, the users and others concerned. Such relations may be qualitative, like the acceptability of the education provided, no less than quantitative, like the relation between the number of places in the schools and the number of children to be accommodated. At the same time, it must keep the total demand of this and all its other services within its total resources of men, money and materials, not to speak of those no less critical and less expansible resources, skill, time and attention. These resources are themselves not a datum but to some extent a function of policy.

The settlement of a budget by such a body involves the comparison of what seem to be disparate values. The process by which their relative priorities are decided and constantly changed is part of the political process. This process is not confined to organs of central and local government. The governing bodies of professions often have to compare proposals which cannot be referred to any one criterion, yet which conflict with each other or compete for limited resources – for example, proposals involving the protection of its members, its professional education, the public interest and its public image. Charitable foundations have to compare applications for grants for diverse purposes, all within their objects. Public corporations are often set by statute multiple tasks, which cannot be resolved into one. Thus the multi-valued choice[2] is a commonplace of corporate, as of individual life.

Everyone knows from personal experience that the control of an individual life, at least in our culture, involves the process I have called 'optimizing-balancing' – the regulation through time of a host of relationships, not all fully attainable, often sharply conflicting, so as to realize an acceptable combination of them with the resources available. The decisions which give effect to this regulative process are what I mean by multi-valued choices. Politics involves the making of multi-valued choices in the area where they have to be collectively made. Later ages may wonder, as other cultures may wonder now, how anyone in a highly developed society like our own can cherish the belief that undertakings operating for profit in a market can escape the embarrassing value judgments inherent in the multi-valued choice.

This belief rests on two assumptions, both of which are even less true today than they used to be. One is the assumption that managing a business can be *fully* described as managing an investment and that therefore *all* the criteria which determine success in business management can be reduced to or derived from those which determine success in managing an investment. The other – a necessary corollary – is that companies operating for profit in a market can leave the multi-valued choosing to the individual buyers, to whom it rightly belongs. The market will convert their manifold priorities into signals which will guide the profit-seeking entrepreneur on the course best calculated to satisfy them, as well as himself – or will eliminate him in favour of rivals who can read the signals better.

Few people today accept these assumptions in the unqualified form which was acceptable to their grandfathers but even fewer, I think, realise how far they have been eroded or how far their residual truth is itself a cultural artifact, subject to cultural change.

They have been eroded by changes in economic conditions. In the free market of classical economics buyers and sellers were so numerous that price was a function of the market, independent of any individual operator. Such markets barely exist today in any important field, whether in goods or services, in foreign exchange or in labour which is only uneasily regarded as a market at all.

These assumptions have also been eroded by political changes. In an ever wider field – for instance, in the land and property market – the preferences and values expressed by individual buyers and sellers represent so small a fraction of the social valuing and preferring which is involved that the missing element is increasingly expressed either by public regulation of the market or by the entry of government, central or local, as buyers or sellers, using market mechanisms to express political choice. An increasing volume of individual needs can be satisfied only by political choice – for example, the need for viable roads, as distinct from automobiles, for viable towns, as distinct from houses. The social costs and values of all activities, public and private, demand entry into a calculus far beyond that of the market. Political choice, which is simply the multi-valued choice of a collectivity, rather than of an individual, takes over increasingly from market choice, as individual choice becomes over-charged with social implications; and thus displaces the market as a calculus of value, even whilst retaining it as a distributive mechanism.

The assumption that business success should be measured solely by the criteria applicable to managing an investment derived its validity – and still derives such validity as it has – from the fact that it was and to some extent still is incorporated in the mores of society. In so far as it is no longer so accepted, the reason is that society has developed wider and different expectations of business; and in consequence, business management, itself an integral part of that society, has responded by accepting these expectations and partly incorporating them in its own standards of success.

And this is just what we should expect, from any just appreciation of the psycho-social nature of societies. If we boggle at the idea in business, whilst we accept it in every other field, it is because the imposing structure of economics conceals from our notice the inadequate model of man adopted by the early economists – inadequate even in their day in its exclusion of his social nature but doubly inadequate today with the change both of market conditions and of social expectations.

This is, in my experience, a fact of common observation. Anyone who has sat on the board of a business corporation will recall the variety of items which come before it. They concern its relations with its staff and employees, its customers and its suppliers, its bankers and its rival colleagues in the trade; with local government, central government and several different public opinions. Although all these are considered for their bearing on the profitable continuance of the business, yet in every field discussion reveals other autonomous standards of expectation entertained not only by others but by the directors themselves about themselves and their undertaking. Their aim is not merely to survive and to grow but to attain and improve on those standards which, in every one of those fields, they have somehow come to regard as standards of success.

There is, indeed, a difference in degree between undertakings operating through the market and those which more directly formulate political choices. To this extent policy decisions in business are usually easier than those on more political bodies. Where growth, as well as survival, is culturally regarded as a major standard of success, metabolic criteria are more pervasive, at least up to whatever level is currently regarded as 'success'. I have already dissented from the idea that in this or any other field success means 'maximizing', rather than 'satisficing'.

Yet I think it well to insist on the ubiquity of the multi-valued choice, in business as elsewhere, because of the dangerous and increasing pressures to mask or ignore it.

It is often masked by concentration on problems of survival. Competitive enterprises are not necessarily less secure than others, nor do they necessarily feel so. (It has been my experience that successful competitive enterprises worry less about money than do most public monopolies, for the simple reason that they often feel rich, whilst public monopolies are carefully guarded from such dangerous euphoria.) Yet the metabolic relations of business undertakings are often more directly a function of their own policy and hence occupy more of their attention. And since they must survive by their own efforts in a necessarily uncertain future, the shadow of insecurity is never far away.

The multi-valued choice is also masked – in all undertakings but most easily in business undertakings – by the fact that all men of action hate it. It involves seeing a situation in more than one way, a conceptual feat difficult in itself and one which also vastly complicates the task of regulation. It is hard enough to keep the manifold variables involved in survival and growth in line with their governing relations. When to these multiple and often conflicting criteria are added functional criteria, requiring judgments which cannot be derived from financial estimates (though of course these must limit them) life for the administrator becomes even harder. Even in government, balancing budgets, realizing surplusses, improving 'efficiency', are often mistaken for standards, rather than mere conditions of success. In business, the traditional authority so to regard them reinforces a powerful natural inclination.

Yet the industrial policy maker shares many of the troubles of his more 'political' counterpart and there is every reason why he should. I once participated in the debate on an industrial board concerned to decide how high to set its target for export, in response to government emphasis that this should be given priority on national grounds. No one doubted that exports could be increased – at a price. Everyone knew, on the other hand, that every increase in export sales at that time would correspondingly reduce home sales, which were several times more profitable and would make it even harder than it then was to keep home delivery dates short enough to retain the business. It would have been easier, safer and more profitable to leave exports as they were; yet no one suggested this course. The struggle for survival was not at the time so fierce as to mask, in the minds of the directors, the other expectations which society had of them; nor would it have done so in the minds of shareholders, consumers or any other of the parties concerned, if they could have been parties to the discussion and the decision.

In fact, one need not look outside the range of metabolic criteria to find the endemic, multi-valued choice. At what point, for example, should stock levels be fixed, so as to secure work against the likelihood of interruption, without locking up more capital than need be? Rival answers appeal to the same metabolic criterion (we may call it maximizing 'profit' or 'worth' or what you will) but no known calculus can derive an answer without weighting dangers and probabilities in a way which we cannot specify and do not understand. Or to take a clearer example, how much of a year's profit should be distributed to shareholders and how much retained in the business? This familiar exercise involves not only the same unspecifiable calculations but also

74

the assessment of conventional standards which are as much a part of the social mores as any other governor of behaviour and are equally a product of the process which they help to direct.

I invite you, therefore, to mute the distinction which we are accustomed to draw between 'political' and commercial policy; to accept the multi-valued choice as endemic in all collective, as in all individual regulation; and to disbelieve every attempt to reduce it, in theory or in practice, to logical deduction from a single criterion.

So far, I have argued this in terms of examples drawn from 'top-level' decision making; but if it is true, it should apply at all levels; and so it does. The girl in charge of a typing pool has to manage a bundle of relationships as disparate in their way and on their scale as those of the managing director. She has to handle a varying work load with a varying staff, in a manner sufficiently acceptable to her various clients (whose expectations and tolerances differ). She has to maintain the morale and the technical standards of her team, satisfy her own standards and keep the demands on herself within her own capacity and standard of acceptability. Each of these different dimensions has along it some point beyond which deviance will beget self-exciting confusion in the sub-system she has to manage. Within these limits her capacities and standards of regulation define the state at which she shall maintain the sub-system for which she is responsible. Her role contains in miniature the whole profile of management.

This also we should expect. Chester Barnard[3] first compared the relation of a corporation with its management team to the relation of the body with the brain and central nervous system. This is a sub-system not separate from the body but part of it, drawing its energy from the body's metabolic processes, dependent on the body for its continued existence; yet none the less regulative of the organism as a whole and capable of directing it on courses sustained through time; courses, incidentally, which may stress, jeopardize, even defeat its own self-maintenance. Since he wrote, communication engineers have designed regulative mechanisms as parts of larger systems, such as space craft and automatic factories, which make his model familiar from another angle.

An organization, like an organism, is a hierarchy of systems. Each is able to act as a whole only because its subordinate systems are so organized as to hang together – as the typing pool continues to function only because the woman in charge knows how to keep it together, even at the cost of staving off demands it cannot safely try to meet. Whatever be the level to which we happen to direct our attention, be it a plant in a large complex, a department of the plant or an office of the administration, we can assume a set of relations internal to it which keep it together and which are separate from and sometimes in conflict with the set of relations which links it inseparably with other sub-systems and with the larger configurations of which it forms part. It is a necessary function of management at any level to remember that many of the relations internal to it are external when viewed from the level of some sub-system on which it depends, a sub-system which has its own stabilities to guard and its own standards of success. These subordinate standards deserve close attention and unceasing respect. For the organization functions as a whole only in so far as its subordinate sub-systems function as wholes. It is no less dependent on them than they on it.

Thus the entire structure is a tissue of mutual expectations systematically organized in mutually supportive sub-systems, governed by standards which are partly self-generated and constantly self-changed. And it is itself linked to the society within which it functions not merely by the mutual expectations of organization and society but by the interlocking and multiple roles of every one of its members, from top to bottom, especially those who form part of the management team.

I am sure that many of you remain convinced that for a business enterprise, survival and growth are the necessary and sufficient criteria of success. True, these are pursued today within limitations more rigorous than existed a few decades ago. Public regulation, public opinion, organized labour and full employment impose on the operator requirements more exacting than his father knew; but the basic condition (you may say) remains unchanged. The operator pursues a unitary standard of success, namely survival and growth, well recognized and accepted by the whole business community, even though he pursues it within the limitations of multiple conditions. Taking this view, you will find me perverse in promoting these conditions to the status of rival standards of success. All other types of organization (you may concede) from governments to charities, exist to perform functions, sometimes multiple and conflicting functions and their success must be judged by themselves and others by reference to such standards of performance as may seem reasonable; but business is happily exempt from such a multivaluational quagmire.

If you take this view, I cannot prove you wrong; and I must defer most of my further persuasion to a further talk (ch. 6). But because survival and growth hold so dominant a place in the evaluation of business success, I will explore them a little further to show that they are neither so unitary nor so precise as they are sometimes supposed to be.

The least questionable status that can be assigned to survival is simply this. Few organizations aspire only to survive – except, perhaps, at moments when their dissolution seems too imminent to leave room for other thoughts. None, on the other hand, can do anything else, unless they do survive. Survival, then, is a universal *condition*, but only occasionally a *standard* (or criterion) of success.

This claim is over-simplified, because it implies that survival and non-survival are 'on-or-off', mutually exclusive states, like life and death, which can be predicated of some clearly definable 'thing' called 'the organization'. The actual position is more complex. Since an organization consists of many overlapping systems, the interest of the regarding mind determines which of them shall be regarded as critical and what degree of discontinuity shall be regarded as 'non-survival'.

For this purpose the legal criterion of liquidation is almost irrelevant. Liquidation incidental to reconstruction may leave unchanged all the significant relations of investors, managers, workers and staff. Conversely, a discontinuity which displaces them all may yet preserve formal continuity of incorporation – and a useful balance of losses, carried over for the benefit of the new owner's tax liability.

Consider *what* survival is threatened by the prospect of three diverse events – liquidation through insolvency; nationalization by compulsory acquisition of assets; and a take-over bid. The first is, potentially, the most radical, since it threatens the continuity of relations deemed critical by investors, managers, employees and creditors alike. But even in this case, the optimum path to 'survival' – more exactly, to preserving as much as possible of what they value most – may differ sharply for each group.

The second involves a dichotomy of a revealing kind. The company is threatened with the loss of its business but not of its capital. Even the business, lost to the company, will be virtually undisturbed. It will continue as a going concern within a larger system. Management may go with the business, retaining continuity of employment through change of employer or may stay with an employer whose business will be new. The investors will retain the substance of an investment which has wholly changed its form. In so complex a metamorphosis it is especially clear that what 'survives' and what does not depends on the position and the value structure of the regarding mind.

The third example illustrates in a different way the difference between legal and sociological realities. In form, the take-over bid invites no more than a voluntary transaction between buyers and sellers of shares. It has no direct effect on management, business or employees. It involves the board only to the extent that their advice will influence the potential sellers and is thus of importance to the potential buyers. In fact, of course, the directors are involved not only or chiefly as disinterested counsellors. Their past policy may be by implication criticised, their future is shadowed by doubt. Whether they will continue in office and if so with what colleagues, under what direct or indirect influence or curtailment of discretion, all this and more is at risk. Of all the relations which matter to them none may survive the change. Nor is the threat purely a personal one. The policies with which they have identified themselves may have become so much a part of the undertaking's character that others beside themselves regard the survival of the business as at stake.

Already several systems have emerged, each of which may be separately threatened. The shareholder's eye and the director's eye select for attention different aspects of the undertaking's activity and group them differently with others which are of concern to them. And each of them may view the company as an investment or a business activity or a social entity or in all these ways and will find different variables critical to each view.

These complexities do not exhaust the manifold systematic views which other eyes may select. Only one of my three examples is likely to threaten the survival of those systematic relations on which almost all the employees depend – the metabolic relations by which work done elicits money earned; the functional relations by which the same activities provide the doer with status, security, support and the opportunity to exercise skill. These sub-systems, however, are constantly threatened by changes which seem far less radical when viewed from the board-room. A minor change in production method may eliminate the whole of one or many such sub-systems, depreciating skills, altering relations and eliminating jobs. These are not less serious or less complex threats to those whom they affect than the threats to the board-room implicit in the take-over bid.

Survival is indeed no simple, unitary, on-or-off concept, to be transferred without qualification from the biological to the business world – even when its biological meaning is understood. In fact, the mythology of capitalism is haunted by evolutionary concepts which biologists outgrew decades ago.

It is still an honoured, if not a well-explored assumption of many business men that survival is not only a condition but an ultimate criterion of success; that every judgment can and should in the last analysis be justifiable as the choice of a best path to that unitary, metabolic goal, enhanced capacity to survive. This makes little sense in terms of evolutionary biology and much less in terms of modern capitalism. Evolution is concerned not with individuals but with species. It produces by elimination not necessarily the fittest but the fit enough – hence its infinite variety. It produces these types step by (usually) irreversible step – hence its 'wastefulness' and 'inefficiency' when judged by the standards to which our culture attaches value. It throws little, if any light on the behaviour even of species during the period, often reckoned in tens of millenia, during which they are disappearing – a state which no doubt includes all but a tiny and unidentifiable fraction of the organizations around us today. Great as has been the contribution of evolutionary theory to human thought, its influence on the myth-ology of capitalism must surely be reckoned on the debit side.

Leaving aside these more ambitious and illusory claims, the preser-vation of *some* set of relationships through time and change remains a condition, though not a criterion of success. I have stressed the mani-fold variety of relations which may be identified with survival not to diminish its importance but to stress its variety and its relativity.

When we turn to the other familiar yardstick, growth, we find the same variety and the same relativity; but the picture is even harder to compress into a small compass, so I will simplify it in terms of what seem to me to be the three main patterns, in terms of which it may be understood.

Consider, first, the relation of the manager to the system which it is his job to regulate. If his capacity is fully taxed, he will welcome any growth which will make his task easier – for example, by increasing the resources available to him in his 'optimizing-balancing' function or by reducing the demands on it – and he will correspondingly avoid growth in any dimension which would have the opposite effect. If on the other hand he is conscious of unused capacities in himself, he will try to expand his job to the limit of his powers. This tendency is com-monly called power-seeking or empire-building. The terms are correct but I avoid them because they carry a pejorative sense which I wish to exclude. Our gratitude, as well as our hate, is chiefly due to power-seekers and empire-builders. The growth of economic, as of political empires is usually due to the initiative of the builders, rather than to any particularly favourable features of their resources or their circum-stances.

This pattern is powerfully affected by another, our cultural attitude to growth. Here, in our present time and place, the main feature is the sharp difference between our attitudes to growth in the public and the private sector. Briefly, growth in the public sector still tends to be suspect and resented, even in fields of obvious and urgent need, whilst growth in the private sector still tends to be accepted and approved, or at least tolerated, even where the activity is widely regarded as futile or dangerous. This cultural pressure strongly modifies the attitudes, as well as the tasks of regulators in the two sectors.

A third pattern, not identical with the second, further affects the other two. This is the institutional pattern by which the resources for growth are generated. The main distinction falls between undertakings which recover their costs from users, members, supporters or subscribers and those which recover them from public revenues by acts of political choice. Private enterprises, charities and many public utilities fall on one side of the line, though the last are usually limited in their facilities for raising or accumulating capital. The rest of government enterprise falls on the other side. Bodies in which membership is in fact unavoidable for those concerned, as in many professional organizations and trade unions provide a curious intermediate case.

Thus the attitude of any manager towards growth as a criterion of success is mainly determined by the interaction of three factors – his own situation in relation to the current regulative state of his organization; the expectations entertained of him by the culture (which to some extent he doubtless shares); and the resources for growth which are available to him.

An unique course of history explains the present patterns in the second and third fields. Briefly, two successful achievements have bred their own reversals. One curbed the irresponsible exercise of political power and harnessed it to the private sector. The other built, within the private sector organs of economic power irresponsible to political control. The huge dichotomy is painfully healing; political power reluctantly accepts economic responsibilities, as economic power reluctantly accepts political responsibilities, each fortified in its reluctance by the cultural values developed in its previous phase.

Against this background, consider very briefly some of the variables in which growth may be seen by different eyes as a criterion of success.

Investors in profit-making enterprises – but not in other enterprises

– rate the success of their investment in terms of increasing profitability and increasing net worth. Managers of profit-making enterprises, however, watch the growth of other indices also. (The old-fashioned entrepreneur, managing a business financed with his own money, did not have to distinguish between the elements of financial and entrepreneurial success; but his usually separate descendants, the investor and the professional manager, have inherited different parts of his estate.) The manager regards as a criterion of success growth in any variable, physical or financial, which enlarges the system he has to regulate (if he is under-stressed) or makes its regulation easier (if he is over-stressed). Changes in the structure of business have added increased value to growth in some of these dimensions. For example, the industrial manager is interested in the growth of those physical variables, notably turnover, which are associated with the economies of mass production; and all managers are interested in the growth of those variables – a wider set – which enable a business to carry a heavier load of overhead expenses and thus of expensive management skills and management aids (for example, computers).

On the other hand, mass production methods and a rising proportion of indirect expenses make businesses more vulnerable to any shortfall in demand below their planned capacity; and this is reinforced by a cultural valuation, dating from the 1930's, that under-employment of resources, especially of human resources need not and should not be tolerated. A system so set, is bound, if it succeeds, to run constantly into the troubles bred of scarce resources and to seek relief in physical growth, each step in which will raise the level not only of what can be used but of what must be used and will thus further speed the process.

This in turn speeds the concern of industry with the expansion and creation of markets. Competing industrialists found out long ago that they had far more to gain from expending their total market than from competing with each other for shares in a static one. (It is rare for any business undertaking to prosper in a shrinking market or to fail to prosper in one which is expanding.) Hence the growing concentration of industry on the promotion of demand, which early economists could simply assume.

Government fans the flame for another reason. Standards of human expectation rise not only in those fields where desire can be satisfied by purchase across a counter but also in areas which must be defined by the political process, provided by the public sector and paid for at the public expense – in education, health, sanitation, public order, roads, transport and so on. And with a growing population, it costs ever more even to maintain these services at levels minimally accept-able by the standards of the past. Clearly, an ever larger slice of the gross national product is needed to satisfy these demands. But a power-ful cultural valuation resists the growth of organization in this sector, however urgently desired its products and however obvious and re-sented its shortcomings, and still more fiercely resists increases in the proportion of the national wealth devoted to it. Since another conven-tional valuation precludes governments from manipulating preferences with the freedom used by operators in the private sector, the growth of the gross national product largely limits the rate of growth in the public services.

These are among the tendencies which have combined to create in Western cultures a self-exciting economic system of the kind we know. One of its effects is to give a central place to growth in the culture's value system and to draw this sharp and curious distinction between its valuation in the private and the public sectors – or, more exactly, between the sector which operates through the market (even though it is in no real sense *regulated* by market forces) and the sector which does not. The manager operating in the sector where growth is favour-ably valued will often find this valuation attached uncritically to growth in variables (especially technological variables) for no better reason than its association with the generally benign view of growth, just as he may find fields in which stability is, for no better reason, equated with stagnation – a powerful example of the power of words to pre-judge issues to which they are applied.

I am not concerned here to criticize these evaluations, still less to criticize them for being evaluations. I am concerned only to point out that they *are* evaluations, judgments made within the framework of a specific culture, themselves disclosures of that culture's setting and influences in its change. Like survival, growth is measured along many dimensions, valued from many standpoints and often adopted as a yardstick for reasons justified only by history or even superficial analogy. Such valuations, their differences and their conflicts are products of our culture, facts but also artifacts, perhaps the highest, certainly the most basic of our mental and social creations, permitting and demanding conscious, as well as unconscious change.

The significance of these conclusions, however, depends on a much closer understanding of the process by which standards of success in the minds of administrators are set and changed by the social process of which they are part. I shall have more to say about this in my next paper.

NOTES AND REFERENCES

[1] I have traced the varieties of organization along this variable in *The Art of Judgment* (ch. 11). (1965) London: Chapman and Hall, and New York: Basic Book: Inc.

[2] I have developed this further in a paper, 'The Multi-valued Choice', in *Communication, Concepts and Perspectives* (edited by Lee Thayer). (1966) Washington D.C.: Spartan Books Inc.

[3] Barnard, Chester J., *The Functions of the Executive*. (1938) Cambridge, Mass.: Harvard University Press.

CHAPTER SIX

What Controls the Controllers?

I HAVE described the managers of an undertaking – *any* undertaking – as regulators of a system or sub-system; concerned to regulate its internal and external relations with a view both to preserving its essential balances and to optimizing the multiple results of its activities. And I have suggested that the standards which determine what relations are to be sought or shunned are largely conventional, set and changed by the society of which the undertaking is a part through a social process to which managers contribute more than most. This view challenges us to find some way of describing the manager's multiple relations which shall be simple enough to use with confidence as a basis for thought and discussion but not so simplified as to ignore essential facts – as, I think, our current ways of thinking generally do.

The least complex approach which does sufficient justice to the facts is, I think to regard the manager in four different ways – as accountable to others; responsive to situations; committed to a role; and possessing initiative. These are related but distinct and in our contemporary culture the third and fourth are often under-valued. I will explore these four approaches and try to show what each contributes to the age-old problem of making power responsible without making it inefficient.

Political history has been greatly concerned with the struggle to make power accountable both to those over whom it is exercised and to those by whom it is delegated. The basic difficulty is that in any social organization powers are inseparable from particular positions from which alone they can be exercised. No one, whether above or below a power-holder in the hierarchy, can manipulate the powers he holds without sitting on the seat he occupies. Whether we think of a political executive, however democratically appointed or a business subordinate, however clearly his delegated powers are defined, once he is in the saddle, he and he alone must exercise the powers and use the discretions which are inseparable from them. The best that political science has been able to do so far is to devise means to replace the power holder by another and to control the resources from which his power derives. These are the two powers which the British constitution has evolved for the protection of the governed. They also describe the formal powers which shareholders have over boards of directors and by which executives hold to account those who are responsible to them.[1]

Of these powers, the second is barely distinguishable from other powers not formally constituted, such as the power of employees to withhold their labour or of buyers to withhold their custom. Indeed, these informal powers are not only identical in effect but often more potent and easier to use than the power of Parliament to withhold supplies or of higher authority to cut a subordinate's budget or to limit his discretion. So I will regard the first only, the power to replace, as the basis of formal accountability. The legal obligation to render an account may indeed exist and be valuable even where the party entitled to demand the account does not possess the right to hire and fire the accounting party; but it is not, I think, too far from common usage to restrict the term 'accountability' to cases where this relationship exists.

The power to replace one man by another in the seats of power, whether political or economic, is a right of great value in at least three ways. It provides a means to determine the succession to power, certainly, quickly and peacefully. It enables those who hold it to rid themselves of a power-holder who is deemed incompetent, irresponsible or otherwise unacceptable. And by its mere existence it establishes those who hold it as people of whose views the power-holder must take account.

The practical effect of these powers, however, depends on the social situation in which they are exercised and on the cultural background shared by the parties to the account. If, for instance, the holders to the account cannot bring themselves to trust the power-holder, whoever he may be, they can hardly fail to render any power-holder impotent and thus to defeat their proper expectations of him. Alternatively, if no competent and trustworthy alternative is available, their right to re-place the existing holder will be valueless. Thus, for the right to be useful, those who hold it must (a) be able to decide whether the power-holder is worthy of continued trust; (b) be willing to accord him trust, until the contrary appears; and (c) be able to choose a better alternative if need be. The 'account' contributes only to the first and even to that much less than is commonly supposed.

The purpose of the account is to inform those to whom it is rendered on all those matters within the competence of the power-holder which are of interest to them; and its scope is as wide or as narrow as those interests may be. These are probably at their widest in the relations of political executive and electorate – how varied are the grounds on which an election may be lost or won! They are much narrower in the relations of directors and shareholders, since the aspects of a busi-ness which are significant to investors are relatively few.

More important, however, than the scope of the account is the amount of relevant information which it can, at best, contain. The holders to account have a set of expectations, wide or narrow, precise or vague, concerning the course of affairs which the power-holder is trying to regulate and the first requirement of the account is that it should tell them whether these expectations have been fulfilled. If so, the holders to account will probably be satisfied. If not, they will have to decide, first, whether the discrepancy really reflects an abnormal course of events, rather than an erroneous setting of their own expect-ations; if so, how far, if at all, this is due to ineffective management by the power-holder; and finally whether to exercise their power of replacement. To guide them in these decisions far more information is needed than they will need if their expectations are met – far more, often, than the account can possibly supply.

The accounting of directors to shareholders, like that of executives to a board of directors and of superiors to subordinates all down the hierarchy, is a link in the feedback system by which each holder to account is enabled to compare the course of events with his expecta-tions; and the signals which it elicits are subject to all the varying de-grees of uncertainty which I have analysed in earlier talks (especially ch. 2). These limitations can best be seen by exploring the most familiar and precise accounting, the annual report and accounts rendered by directors to shareholders. The formal relation of the parties to this account is financial and the accounts which they render are in a form which law and custom have evolved over the years to match the limited and measurable variables with which they are concerned. The board is expected to carry on business with the capital entrusted to it; to preserve and increase this; to earn an acceptable profit on it; and to distribute an acceptable proportion of this in dividend. The standards of what is acceptable in each of these dimensions is set, as I have argued, by a social process. Whatever their origin, they are sufficiently clear at any time to measure success; and if they disclose conventional success, there is little to add by way of report. Generally speaking, the better the accounts, the shorter the report can be.

Such judgment by results is at best a rough, statistical procedure, reliable only in certain conditions which are often absent. Any year, however good its results, may have included ruinous errors of management, the results of which have not yet become apparent. To be evidence of success, results must extend over a period long enough to span the normal interval between major decisions and their results; and comparable undertakings in the same field must provide standards of comparison. Yet even when these conditions are most imperfectly met, their absence will probably go unnoticed, so long as results reveal no alarming disparites with expectation.

If, however, the results are disappointing, far more information is required than the financial accounts can disclose. Some of this the directors will supply in the report. They will give their explanation of the untoward course of events. They will describe what they did to minimize its effects. They will put forward their plans and estimates for the future. The shareholders must decide whether to continue or withdraw their confidence, even whether to revise their expectations of what should be regarded as success; and in doing so, they must use mental processes far beyond those involved in the simple cycle of control with which control mechanisms have made us familiar. The mis-match signal in such a situation is no more than a provisional red light, inviting

88

a new appreciation of the situation. If they decide to use – or not to use – the powers they have, the decision will have been selected not by the original mis-match signal generated by the account but by another, generated by that appreciation.

Where the accounting party is one whose standards of success are not expressed in money, the holders to account are likely to find themselves regularly in the position which shareholders of trading undertakings meet only in bad years. For example, an increase in the revenues of a central or local government is not of itself, in our culture, a source of satisfaction to the generality of citizens who provide it (though it may be so to those who have the spending of it). To the citizens the measure of success is the quality of the service provided, relative to the felt need on the one hand and the cost on the other. Both these standards are matters of judgment, only partially open to objective confirmation; and the quality of the service actually provided is equally hard to relate to measurable criteria. The 'holding to account' can therefore only take the form of an on-going political debate, in which financial information plays only a small part, though one often larger than it deserves.

The difficulty appears even more sharply in a charity concerned to raise money and apply it in a charitable cause. Its supporters reckon success partly in the increase of its revenue; but like the citizen, their basic interest is in the furtherance of the cause. They are thus mainly interested in how the money is spent and the philosophy of the market supplies a much weaker assurance that growth in itself means good performance – even though charities, as money-raisers, are as fiercely competitive as any trading enterprise, in their efforts to increase their share of what the public can be persuaded to give away. So the controllers of the charity must justify themselves to their supporters, both as money-raisers and as money-spenders.

Public corporations also cannot rely on financial accounts as an index of their success. Even though they are required by the State to earn a given return on their captial, their success in doing so is seldom evidence of their success in achieving their statutory objects. It shows at best only the attainment of one out of many conditions of success. The fact that such corporations usually keep their accounts in the same form as commercial undertakings does not of itself make these accounts any more informative, though it may give the illustion, dangerous though sometimes useful, that it does so.

A classic example occurred when the British coal industry was nationalized. The Act which gave effect to this required the new board, in brief, to organize the industry, get the coal and satisfy the consumer. At that time no clear or agreed standards existed in the minds of any of the parties, defining what in any of these fields should be deemed to constitute success, though everyone knew that the state of affairs in all three fields, when the industry was taken over after the war, fell short of any acceptable standard by a margin which could not be overtaken for some years.

How best to organize a thousand pits in twenty-two diverse coal-fields? At what rate, in their different conditions, could production and productivity be expected to increase? How should the limited talent available be distributed between current production, short-term development and new sinkings? What pricing policy would best satisfy the needs of many categories of consumer, competing for a variety of coals, each gotten at most varied costs? It was possible to supply descriptive information on what seemed to the board the relevant aspects of these and many other problems and the reasons for the answers adopted. To devise standards by which the holders to account could assess the success of its new servant was more difficult; but it was not beyond the powers of informed people to reach a rough concensus.

The item most clearly irrelevant to this judgment, in the early years, was the relation of revenue to expenditure. As a monopolist responsible for abating a national energy famine, the board's declared policy was to maximize production and sell it as cheaply as would cover the costs of production. Even this policy did not suffice to avert, though it helped to minimize some critical energy shortages.

The price was fixed far below the level which market forces would have permitted. This was a political decision. The decision could be – and was – debated; but given the decision, the resultant balance of revenue and expenditure threw no light whatever on the extent to which the board were succeeding or failing in their new tasks. Yet so strong was the traditional meaning attached to profit and loss that year after year it was the first and often the only feature to be seized on for praise or blame, even by responsible commentators. The report had an exciting story to tell, inviting judgment on great issues closely affecting every citizen in the land. Yet nothing, it seemed, could break the conviction that this magic figure, black or red, *must* signify success or failure and that any effort to set up other criteria *must* be not only vain but a dangerous escape from economic 'realities'.

Thus those to whom the controllers of undertakings are accountable do not necessarily learn from the accounts or even from the report what they need to know about the variables in which success is measured; and even when they do, they cannot learn from it and may not learn from elsewhere the standard by which success in that variable should be measured. And when, rightly or wrongly, they are disappointed, they cannot assume that the controller is at fault. The cause may lie in an erroneous setting of their own expectations or in changes in the course of events with which the controller has dealt as well as anyone could have done. Only a further enquiry of a different sort can interpret the red light or even determine the validity of its apparent redness.

The same problem faces an executive, valuing the performance of a subordinate. So long as expectations are not disappointed, confidence is not shaken and no question arises. When expectations are not met, the alerting signal does not of itself condemn the subordinate. It merely puts the superior on enquiry into a situation of which this signal may be only a peripheral symptom. The resulting mental process – an elaborate simulation of the entire situation from the assumed point of view of the subordinate – is one of which we know little, though it is subjectively familiar. Analogue and digital computers cannot yet model the complex simulations which in such situations we habitually construct in our heads; but at least they make it scientifically respectable (for the first time) to credit ourselves with the ability to make them.

Thus the powers of those who can hold to account, though important, are awkward to use and limited in value; and they would be of even less use than they are, if they were not reinforced by a network of responsiveness, pervading and supplementing them, which comes into view when we consider the manager in the other three capacities which I distinguished earlier. To realize how pervasive these are, let any power-holder ask himself – 'Of whose expectations need I take account in exercising my powers?' At once there springs into view an immense nexus of expectations, from superiors, subordinates and colleagues, from employees, suppliers and customers, from everyone with whom his role or any associated role links him in any relationship. Each of these defines what some 'other' will expect of him as an acceptable standard of performance. Of some of these he must take account to avoid the repercussions of disappointing them; and in doing so he acts in the way I have described as responding to a situation. Of most of them he must take account because he accepts them as inherent in his role; and in doing so, he acts as one committed to a role. There are yet others of which he takes account because he expects them of himself, even though no one but himself would be disappointed, if they were left unfulfilled, In so far as he sets himself, within his role, these private standards of success, he exercises that initiative in norm-setting which I distinguished as the fourth capacity in which we need to view him – and incidentally, sets in motion a process which will soon affect the expectations of others and may permanently change the role he plays.

I will briefly discuss these three forms of control.

Responsiveness to situation is a familiar way of explaining human behaviour – a scientifically respectable way also, since it is not distinctively human but can be demonstrated in other creatures in the laboratory and observed in the field. Not only the battle but the bargain and the compromise can be explained in such terms. Games theory refines the logical calculation of 'best' issues, in interactions between creatures, each informed of what is 'best' for itself.

In fact, however, political and economic behaviour in human societies have many features which are unique to them. A model based purely on response to situation would not represent more than a fraction of what happens. It would not even explain how accountability comes to be accepted. As governors of behaviour roles are of paramount importance and some aspects of them have not yet, I think, received due attention, especially in business.

Although in all societies established roles supply the principal basis for prediction, mutual trust and co-operative action, they have usually in the past been attached to traditional positions in the social structure, positions to which individuals are born or succeed by traditional procedures – the roles, for instance, of father, husband, warrior, chief. When industrial societies made the transition which Maine described as 'from status to contract', they would have disintegrated (even more than they did) if the contractual obligations of newly designed posts had not been quickly and imperceptibly expanded into social roles.

The contract which appoints a man a manager imposes on him the obligations to meet all the expectations which others 'properly' entertain of a holder of that role; and similarly confer on him so far as a contract can do so, the right to expect from others whatever such a role-holder may 'properly' expect. Organizations subsist, despite changes in personnel, only to the extent that their members assume that a role-holder, personally unknown to them and perhaps known to be new to the job, will be governed by his role, both in what he will try to do and in what he will regard as being debarred to him; and this in turn depends on common agreement on what is 'proper' to the role.

This development of contractual roles is a major social invention. In the perspective of history it is most unusual that a power-holder, unrestrained by traditional roles, should not use his power to enrich himself, help his friends and destroy his enemies. In many countries today, where industrialization is partial and recent, the solidarity of the extended family makes the claim of each kinsman on all a far more potent moral imperative than the novel requirements of, say, a manager's role that a vacant job be given to the most competent applicant, rather than to the nearest relative. To establish novel roles embodying expectations inconsistent with those built in to time-honoured and established ones is an innovation; and still more radical an innovation is the conception of roles to which anyone may be appointed and in which no one is secure. Our culture depends on such roles to an extent which would surprise a sociologist bred in a different tradition. (Unhappily there are, as yet, few if any sociologists who have been bred in a different tradition.) This fact makes Western industrial discipline, still more Western industrial 'democracy' (such as it is), almost as tender a plant for export as political democracy on the Westminster model. Even within Western countries we can note marked differences – sometimes with envy. The pattern of the future is far from clear.

Whatever be the pattern of the future, the main control to which controllers are subject is and is likely to remain control by role. Accountability is more conspicuous, because it implies a potent sanction; and until recently the regularities of human behaviour were supposed largely to depend on laws enforceable by sanctions. During the last fifty years or so, jurists have learned to revise their views on this and it is useful to give some attention to the change, because it is strictly analogous to changes which we are making (even more slowly) in our understanding of industrial roles.

If jurists have moved faster than economists in assimilating what sociologists have been able to tell them in recent decades, the reason, I think, is not far to seek. To jurists the findings of sociology offered answers to some intractable problems, whilst to economists they threatened disturbance of some established and convenient assumptions. The intractable problems were – 'What makes laws binding?' and 'How do laws grow?'

For some time legal theory had attributed the binding force of a law to the sanction by which it was enforced and had distinguished law from other conventions by the fact that it was enforceable by sanction. It was obvious, however, that sanctions are an indirect and imperfect means of enforcing a rule and that the frequency with which sanctions are employed is a measure of the degree to which a law is *failing* to bind. On the other hand, legal history records cultures in which legal decisions have been sought and valued, even though the public power has no sanction with which to enforce them. Even a sanction operates

not merely to deter would-be law-breakers through fear of conse-
quences but also to reinforce the importance of the rule in the estima-
tion of society and thus to increase its socially binding force. Thus the
making of explicit legal rules and the attachment to them of sanctions
came to be seen as an inseparable part of a much wider process by
which societies accept and adjust the norms by which they live.

This was only one aspect of the enlightenment which in the last half-
century has begun to relieve the darkness of nineteenth century indi-
vidualism. Minds still haunted by the idea of a social contract could not
hope to arrive at any true notion of the function of law, for they had
implicitly assumed that men could be human before they were social.
Only when they had accepted the priority of the social process which
humanizes (more or less) each succeeding generation could they seek
within it the place of law-making and law enforcement.

This in turn made possible a realistic approach to the problem – 'How
does the law grow?' In Britain and North America, which prided themselves on the possession of a Common Law, the growth of this body of
rules by the mere process of use seemed not only a puzzle but even a
scandal; for if the emerging law was 'new' and was not made by Parliament, it must be made by judges; and it seemed strange and offensive
to some minds that judges should make, as they went along, the rules
which they were supposed to be applying. This seemed inconsistent
both with the assumption that every layman is supposed to know the
law and with the principle that Parliament is the source of all law-
making. Extraordinary mental gymnastics were performed to avoid
giving the obvious facts this unwelcome interpretation.

It is clear today that these anxieties derived from a misunderstanding
of the nature of language and thought. Rules of law, like other rules,
apply to classes of situation. The decision whether a particular situation
does or does not fall within a class not only decides a particular case but
also enriches and further defines the class. The categories of the law –
contract, negligence, murder and so on – are open-ended categories,
incomplete and logically incapable of being completed; constantly developed by the process of being used; and at every usage changing,
however slightly, the possibilities of their further development. So are

all the other categories by which we order experience. The growth of the common law by its own progressive application to the changing facts of life is our most conscious and best documented example of the creative element in basic mental and social process.

Organizations, however 'artificial' their nature, however specific their official purpose and however recent their creation, are societies and part of the society in which they arise. Like all societies, they are governed by a net of mutual expectations; if they were not so governed, they could neither hang together nor function as a whole. The process by which these expectations are set and changed is not basically different from the process by which the governing expectations of other kinds of society are set and changed.

It is the openness, the inherent imprecision of roles which leaves open the scope for individual initiative in designing and changing them, in particular, the initative of the role-holder himself. This initative can be exercised in at least two dimensions – in the structure of the role itself and in the concept of success which is pursued within it. A manager may be criticized for acting outside his role or ignoring some of its aspects; and in such cases he is usually described as irresponsible. Equally, though acting fully within his role, he may be judged incompetent. (It is noteworthy that people commonly agree in their judgments of irresponsibility far more than in their judgments of incompetence.) In both dimensions change is constantly at work in the standards of judgment. The scope of a role may change – a manager today is expected to concern himself with a far wider variety of relations than were his concern a few decades ago. Equally, what he tries to accomplish within his role may change. And both kinds of change may be initiated by the role-holder himself. Indeed, such initiative is one of the things which is or should be expected of him.

Thus the growth in responsibility of power-holders is not to be explained wholly as their response to pressures from their surround, whether from those to whom they are accountable or from others who can create situations of which they must take account or even from roles designed for them by others. They themselves have played and should play a part – perhaps the most important part of all – in setting the system which they regulate, including their own roles.

Their capacity for doing so is enhanced by the fact that they are members of more than one system, more than one society. For example, if the standards of care and skill in any profession or craft or the ethics of any profession or skill are to be developed and safeguarded, this is normally achieved only by the interaction and mutual influence of the leaders of the profession, rather than by their clients or by their non-professional chiefs or employers, none of whom can usually make an informed judgment. Imitation and emulation are at least as potent psychic forces as the fear of kicks or the desire for carrots; and their importance becomes more obvious in a society which aspires to minimize the distribution of kicks and even slightly to equalize the distribution of carrots.

We know far less than we need to know about the ways in which standards of success are set but we can confidently assign a major place in the process to individual initiative. Few role-holders leave their roles as they found them. Exceptional men often leave roles too exacting for their successors to fill. (One of the endemic difficulties of organization is to keep the demands of each role within the competence of those who are likely to be available to fill it.) Every role-holder has his own idea of his role and of what, within it, he should regard as success. These ideas are not deviations from some standard pattern; they are part of the stuff from which the pattern is woven and the individual role-holder is perhaps the most important single contributor to the design, since for him, more than for anyone else, it is part of his personal pattern.

Combining the four viewpoints which I proposed at the beginning of this paper, I conceive the power-holder in whatever organization he functions, as primarily a role-holder, exercising the powers which the expectations of others accord to his office, or, more generally, to him in all his capacities. To aid them in assessing his performance, he is usually under some obligation, formal or informal, to render an account of his stewardship, at least to some of them, an obligation which may benefit a much wider circle than those to whom the account is formally owed. (Thus a company's report and accounts are a communication not only to shareholders but to rivals, customers, employees and potential investors and they have to be carefully settled with all these often conflicting publics in mind.)

Some of those with whom the power-holder is in relationship have power to remove him from office. Others have power to make other situations which can force him to attend to their views. He in turn has powers, varying with the situation, to ignore or put 'situational' pressure on these others. Through this mutual relationship, the power-holder receives stimulus and restraint, designed and undesigned, conscious and unconscious, which have the effect of modifying both his actions and his expectations; and so do all those in relationship with him.

The mutual influence of the parties, however, goes much further than this – how much further varies widely with the culture. In so far as the power-holders' satisfactions include the meeting of other people's expectations, signals that he has failed to do so operate as mis-match signals within his own controls, no less than the disappointment of any of his other expectations; and in so far as he expects *of himself* what the others expect of him and shares their judgment of shortcoming, the effect on him is the greater. If such controls seem to us unduly refined or intrinsically weak, let us blame the oddity of our own peculiar culture. In most cultures it would be exceptional, in some inconceivable, for an individual to be indifferent to the expectations which others of his society entertain of him or even not to share the same expectations. The human capacity for thus 'taking the role of the other' is one of the features which distinguish human communication from simple response to a situation. It is observable. Must we disregard it until we can model to ourselves the precise development of brain function to which we owe it?

For a small and extreme but illuminating example, let me return to the charity already referred to. In the case which I have in mind, a small group of concerned laymen and scientists formed a charitable body to collect and dispense funds in what seemed to them a neglected area of research. They formed a small executive group to manage the

charity's affairs and a separate committee, called the research committee, to screen applications and make grants. The body had at first no
members, except the two committees and was entirely self-perpetuat-
ing and formally accountable to no one. In due course it changed the
formal situation by co-opting a council, of which it became a committee and vesting in the council the power to appoint and remove the
committee. The council had no further function and continued to be
appointed by its own executive committee. The research committee
was formally a sub-committee of the executive committee, but appointed its own members, subject to the formal approval of the executive committee.

On the face of it, these two committees were as little accountable
and as independent of control as such bodies could well be. Yet in fact
both committees were subject to informal control more searching than
operates in many bodies of far greater apparent accountability.

There exists in Britain, among those who are rich enough to be repeated targets for charitable appeals, well-defined standards of expectation concerning the right way to run a charity – for example, concerning the maximum proportion of funds raised which should be spent
on fund-raising, the information which should be given, the extent to
which appeals should compete in the same field and so on. The members of the executive committee belonged personally to the world
which applied these standards and they were responsive to its expectations, just as it was responsive to the assurance implied by the association
of their names with the appeal.

Similarly, there exists in Britain among scientists who may seek research grants for themselves or their assistants standards of expectation
concerning the way to support research – the methods of screening and
comparing applications, the means of avoiding bias, the quality of
application which merits support and so on. The members of the research committee were scientists who belonged personally to the world
which applied these standards, and they were responsive to its expectations, just as it was responsive to the assurance implied by the association of their names with the committee responsible for these things.

Not only the report and accounts of the body but its every published action were communications addressed not only or even primarily to its council or even to its supporters but to the whole of the two communities on which it depended for success – on the one hand, the community of potential supporters, on the other, the community of potential users. Each committee was linked to its appropriate public in a sensitive mutual rapport, depending not at all on any legal structure but on the sociological structure of the greater society of which it was a part.

NOTE

[1] Since this went to press Professor Adolph Lowe has pointed out to me that I have taken no account here of those 'checks and balances' on which the American constitution relies. I welcome this comment and note that the checks and balances which were so conspicuously absent in earlier industrial organization are now multiplying, in the statutory and non-statutory powers of organized labour, government and government-sponsored institutions, such as industrial courts.

PART TWO

CHAPTER SEVEN

Stability Control and Choice*

I AM GRATEFUL to those who have done me the honour of asking me to give this address. I am also diffident, for I am conscious of being a stranger to the disciplines of the Faculty which has invited me. I approach my subject not as a scientist but as a layman, turning to science in search of the tools which he needs for his work.

These tools include abstract concepts. Faculties of applied science, such as the one to which I owe my presence here, testify to the unity of thought which links the answering of practical questions with the pursuit of abstract enquiries. So I need not apologize for giving an abstract title to an enquiry into a practical problem.

The problem is briefly this. Engineers organize physical processes; they also organize the productive activities of men. They have recently made great strides in their knowledge of how to organize physical processes so as to be self-regulating. They can build controls which will maintain the operations of a factory or the temperature of a building or the course and stability of an aircraft. The result of these arrangements is that the assembly does what the situation requires without being pushed about by some higher authority. Now this is exactly what engineers in their capacity of managers want to achieve in organizing people. So it is worth enquiring whether what they learn as engineers can help them as managers.

On the face of it, the problems are very similar. The plant manager, for example, has the familiar problem of maintaining stocks of materials at a level high enough to prevent any hold-up in production, yet not so high as to lock up capital needlessly or involve an unacceptable risk

*The ninth Wallberg Lecture – given at the University of Toronto in October 1956.

if prices drop. This is the problem of maintaining stable volume or pressure with a variable throughout, which, as an engineer, he has encountered dozens of times in the control of physical processes; and it is soluble in the same way. A fall or rise in the stock of this or that below or above appointed limits must set buyers buying or stop them buying as surely as a Watts governor opens or closes a valve.

As a general manager, the engineer looks outward at an environment of largely unpredictable and uncontrollable variables – customers, suppliers, competitors, prices, tariffs, freight rates; and he looks inward at his undertaking, a complex, dynamic whole, surviving only by adjustment to forces which it cannot modify; and he sees problems very like those which he had to solve when he was designing automatic pilots for aircraft. The only apparent difference here, as in the control of the inventory, is that the critical elements which open or shut, act or remain inactive, say 'yes' or 'no', are not cogs or holes in cards or electronic valves or what not but – men.

Now the sad thing is that, as our engineer progresses up the ladder of authority, reputation, salary and the other indices of success, he almost certainly becomes, as a controller, progressively less successful. As a plant manager, he will probably not be able, at least in my country, to keep the inventory down to the prescribed limits without periodically using his personal authority; though of all the processes which he controls that would seem as easy as any to make 'automatic'. There will be days when he longs to be back in the research and development department, designing electronic assemblies out of completely reliable units, endowing each with as much discretion as he wishes and no more and confident that each will do what is expected of it, not now and then or nearly always but always. On such days he will regard his fellow men as faulty circuits, unpunchable cards – or worse.

This is likely to be a mistake. In the days when our minds were dominated by mechanical analogies, industry was inclined to think of men as cogs in a machine. It is probably no less misleading to think of them as relays. Happily, science today is less prone to seek a lowest common denominator for all that it observes.

Physics nowadays is concerned with energy rather than with matter, with form rather than substance, with organization rather than with structure, with process rather than with state. The difference between the inorganic and the organic world seems to be largely the difference between relatively closed and open energy systems. The whole world of experience begins to look like a hierarchy of systems; and the main task of science to formulate the laws by which these systems maintain themselves and by which they interact. These changes seem to me to open the way to a better relationship between physics, biology, psychology and the social sciences, that is, between the concepts which we use in trying to understand the processes of matter, of life, of mind and of society.[1]

There is no reason to suppose that the laws of organization which account for the atom and the star will be sufficient to account for the cell and the elephant, let alone the human being and the Ontario Hydro-Electric Power Commission. On the contrary, there is every reason to think that these new forms have come into being through the emergence of new capacities for self-organization. So I am by no means saying that the empire of physics is on the way to absorb the sciences of life and mind. I am only expressing the belief that we are not far from developing new concepts which may be common to the natural sciences and the humanities. Should this prove true, it would simplify the education of engineers, who must somehow learn to span the whole gamut.

So I propose first to look very sketchily at the main levels of organization which we can discern, to see whether they help us to understand the organizations which we ourselves create. Then I will examine the principles which we use in the control of physical processes, to see what bearing they have on the control of organizations. Then I will roughly chart what seems to be the field where choice is not effectively governed by control.

We have been accustomed to think of things as existing, apart from what they do – as a motor car remains a motor car, whether in the garage or on the road. It seems that this is a bad habit. An atom can only be described in terms of activity; and this is equally true of an organism and an organization. Asking about any such thing, 'What is it?', we must divide the question into two to get a useful answer. We must ask, 'How does it hold together?' and 'How does it interact with its environment?' This, incidentally, seems to me to be one of those fruitful concepts which may help to provide sciences at present disparate with a common approach.

The answers will overlap and they will not be simple; for we shall find that, just as the entity we are examining is an integration of activities rather than an assembly of parts, so it is itself more or less integrated into a larger whole. Both scientists and philosophers are concerned to find a better way to represent to ourselves this hierarchy of overlapping systems, within which the things we recognize have both different kinds and different degrees of 'wholeness'. Until they succeed, we can use only a few broad distinctions.

I have not yet seen Niagara; but I understand that, when I do, I shall certainly regard it as 'something'. I shall remember it and recognize it again. This striking and enduring form, this 'steady state', is in substance as transient as a flame. If I ask a scientist, 'What is it?' he will explain it to me in terms of the shape of the river bed, itself partly the work of the river and in terms of the laws which govern the movements and interactions of molecules of water.

But if I ask him what a molecule of water is, he will describe a system of atoms in equilibrium, a closed system, held together by forces of a different order. And if I lead him to discourse on molecular organization in general, he will perplex me with crystals and viruses and arrive in no time at the cell, which organizes itself in a different way and has developed some strikingly new forms of behaviour. It is an open system, maintaining itself by constant interchange with its environment; it is excitable; it grows, reproduces itself, repairs itself, is capable of decay. It has all the characteristics of the organic world.

We have already encountered three types of organization – closed systems; systems like Niagara, which are open to the exchange of matter and energy with their surround; and systems which, even at the cellular level, are also open to information. It is strange that we still have no accepted words to distinguish the last two; still less to distinguish a hierarchy of 'dynamic-information' systems according to their progressive capacity for communication. If we regard these systems as an ascending order, we must remember that higher entities are those which are capable of higher *as well as* lower types of organization. Men in a crowd often behave like water drops; but water drops never behave like men.[2]

As we go up the scale of multi-cellular organisms we notice a very rapid growth in the scale of internal relations and a much slower growth in external relations.

External relations are rudimentary in creatures which have not yet got a central nervous system. You really need a brain to make anything of external relations – and even then the results are not always much to be proud of. But internal relations are another matter altogether. Creatures with no nervous system at all can elaborate faultlessly from a single cell a differentiated, self-maintaining structure which needs myraids of cells to complete; and in doing so they seem to follow a pattern, the nature of which is still a mystery.[3]

In external relations we can note progress in at least three dimensions. The creature becomes able to do a greater variety of things; able to do the same thing in a greater variety of ways; and able to act coherently over a greater span of time.

Compare, for example, the central heating systems of stars, dogs and men. Most stars, I understand, are believed to maintain their inner temperature at about thirty-five million degrees Fahrenheit. If we ask 'How?' and 'Why?', the answer is – 'Because that is the temperature at which the supply of energy and the loss of energy through radiation balance.' At a lower temperature, the nuclear reactions at the centre would be reduced, whereupon – I quote Von Weizsäcker[4] – '. . . the region around the centre of the star could no longer support the pressure from the outside regions. It would be compressed further and thereby its temperature would be raised. The process in the centre . . . would be accelerated by the increase of heat to such a degree that the balance of energy would be restored.'

If we ask why the warm-blooded animals also maintain a constant inner temperature at the more modest level of a little below one hundred degrees Fahrenheit, the answer is – 'Because that is the temperature required by the metabolic processes on which they depend.' But if we ask – 'How?', we receive a much more complicated answer. The creature has a whole battery of resources. Some are physiological; it erects its coat, constricts its surface blood vessels. Some are morphological; it grows a thicker coat. Some, significantly, are behavioural; it huddles together with its fellows or comes to the fire. The means to be used will be determined by something within the creature, rather than by something in the environment. They have a choice of means.[5] But the goal is fixed; it was fixed millions of years ago, when the species took the evolutionary path which gave it this precarious enlargement of scope.

If we ask how and why men centrally heat their houses, we find that the field of choice has widened in two ways. They have immensely enlarged their behavioural responses; and they have come to direct these to goals not biologically determined but chosen from among an immense number of possibilities. Their activities have become more complex and more individual.

We can describe a simple creature wholly in terms of the activity which seems to keep it and its species alive. (At least, we think we can. I am not sure how far we are right.) But when we say of a man that he likes to spend his holidays collecting alpines or of a company that it has decided to go in for producing titanium in a big way, we are describing an activity which is not inherent in men or business corporations as such. Yet once they are committed to it, the new activity becomes characteristic of them, so that a description of them which missed it would be incomplete. They have become differentiated from their fellows by a specific pattern of activity.

It remains to notice those forms which arise from the association of living creatures with others of the same kind and with their ecological milieu. Within some limited habitat, such as a forest or a pond, life finds and holds a dynamic balance; and if disturbed (as we often disturb it by our intervention) it will find another, often after readjustments more far-reaching than we expect. Within this pattern the association of creatures of the same kind ranges from loose and transient associations, through the mutual dependence of the herd to the integration of the hive. At one extreme they are little more than crowds; at the other, little less than organisms.

Generally speaking, associations of creatures are more like crowds than like organisms; and when they approach the internal relations of an organism, as the social insects do, they pay the same price in rigidity and irreversible specialization. Humans alone manage to associate in ways which are elaborate and yet flexible and reversible. Our ability to do so falls far short of our need and we are forever oscillating between two alternatives which seem mutually exclusive – on the one hand, collective efficiency, won at the cost of individual frustration; on the other, individual freedom equally frustrated by collective anarchy. Those who believe in a middle way which is more than a compromise do so in the faith that human beings are capable or can become capable of social organization which is both individually satisfying and collectively effective. It seems fairly clear that this if true is valid only within a certain range of conditions which we cannot yet define.

When we set out to shape our institutions – even to form a company – we are not creating order out of chaos. We are intervening in a dynamic situation already regulated by its own laws. When we propose new goals and establish new organizations to pursue them, the success of our intervention depends on obedience to the same laws which determine whether other societies hold together. We cannot elude the laws of dynamic balance, in government or in management, any more than in engineering. Only so far as we understand and obey them, can we establish self-maintaining configurations of forces of our own devising.

All human institutions are hard to think about. If we personalize them, regarding a nation, a church, a trade union, as if it were a person, we are led into mistaken notions of how they work. If, on the other hand, we regard these names as mere symbols for ways in which people behave, then something essential escapes us. The fact is that we know little about them, as we soon find when we try to answer the two questions into which, as I have suggested, the question – 'What is it?' should be resolved.

How does an institution hang together? I find it convenient to regard institutions as structures of mutual expectation, attached to roles which define what each of its members shall expect from others and from himself. I distinguish them from organisms because they seem to me to hang together in a different way. The cells of an organism are subordinated to the whole by a complete and irreversible division of function which has no parallel in the relation of organisms with each other except among some of the social insects. The members of a human institution, on the other hand, are related by three main modes of interaction which we know as co-operation, conflict and competition.[6] These admit of more precise definition than they usually receive and I believe that all three are needed to maintain that dynamic balance which, in societies no less than among other forms, is the condition of survival; but we know dangerously little about what they mean and how they work.

Institutions grow, repair themselves, reproduce themselves, decay, dissolve. In their external relations they show many characteristics of organic life. Some think that in their internal relations also human institutions are destined to become increasingly organic, that human co-operation will approach ever more closely to the integration of cells in a body. I find this prospect unconvincing – not only, I hope, because I find it unpleasant – for reasons which I will not try to develop now.[7]

Thus human institutions are a distinct and confusing type of entity, built of interactions which range from the human to the mechanical. Among these, business corporations have a peculiar status. Unlike most human institutions, they are planned from the beginning and planned round their external relations, in that they exist to produce a product, to serve a purpose, to make a profit. Yet they depend on the most complex division of internal responsibility. They require of their members close co-operation and elaborate subordination; yet they are not served by a 'natural' society but by individuals who are freely recruited and are free to go, a transient society, of which the members are moved by individual motivations, probably quite foreign to those of the enterprise and have the main focus of their loyalties elsewhere. Yet these strange bodies often attain a high degree of self-regulation, both internally and externally.

I have spent some time in painting the picture of self-regulation as it exists at all levels which we can observe; for here alone we get a glimpse of the laws involved in control; and it is within the realm of these laws that management functions.

In analysing the idea of control I think we can learn from the theory and design of man-made control devices, not because their methods of working necessarily parallel those of the brain or the board-room but because they help us to understand the underlying principles.

I distinguish between two kinds of control, which I shall call positive and negative control. The distinction deserves, I think, more attention than it usually receives. Positive control is a means whereby courses are chosen and kept so as to reach goals. Negative control is a means whereby courses are changed so as to escape threats. They differ in important ways. I want first to discuss positive control.

The helmsman reads from the compass from moment to moment the actual direction of the ship's head, compares it with the course set by the navigator and turns the wheel accordingly. The wheel moves the rudder, directly or indirectly. The effect of the rudder movement, along with all the other influences which affect the ship's course, is reflected after a brief delay on the compass card and the information thus 'fed back' to the helmsman, moves him to a further adjustment of the wheel. In this familiar example of a control circuit the place of the helmsman can easily be taken by an automatic pilot and the design of such a device makes explicit what the helmsman actually does.

The automatic pilot measures both the amount of the deviation and the rate of change. It may have to measure the rate of change of the rate of change, if it is to initiate a stabilizing response. For it is concerned with a continuing process and it must derive from the past enough information to guide it in action which will take effect in the future, even though the delay be very small.

This example yields what seems to me to be the main features of control.

First, there must be a course, an 'ought-to-be', which the control can compare with the actual. If the course is not given, the control must be able to find it, either directly as the homing missile senses the target or by applying built-in rules or by experience. This course, like the actual with which it is compared, usually has a time dimension, being expressed in terms of change (or constancy) with time. The difference between the 'is' and the 'ought-to-be' is the signal for action. Such signals can occur only when the control is in a position to make the comparison. In the example given, the stream of signals is continuous but this is an ideal which is seldom attained. The control may be only intermittently aware of the actual or of the right course; and it can give the signal only when the two are present together.

Next, the assembly under control must be able from the signal to select and make an apt response. This implies, of course, that it has an apt response, which is by no means to be assumed. Here too a time element enters in; for it will take time to make the response and the response must be apt to the situation which will exist, when the response becomes effective. Thus, the A.A. gun predictor must lay off the gun to allow for the movement of the target while the shell is in flight. It must also compensate for the momentum which the gun will generate as it swings.

Finally, news of the situation as modified by the response has to get back to the control to provide the basis for further action. What I have described as 'actual' is in fact past. The helmsman reads the compass 'now' but the rate of change is derived from the recent past and has not yet taken account of rudder movements which are happening 'now'. In most control situations the delays involved are far greater.

Clearly problems of control are haunted by a complicated time factor. Each signal presents information derived from the past and initiates action which will take effect in the future. The effect of the action, more or less masked by other variables, will return for judgment at a still more remote point of time. Thus control is possible, even theoretically, only within limits; and these may present themselves as thresholds which are passed suddenly.

Psychologists have a device called the tracking test. The subject watches a window, across which there unrolls an irregularly wavering track, formed by two parallel lines. With a hand-wheel he has to keep a pointer between the two lines. He has no difficulty, so long as he can see enough of what is coming; but as the speed increases or the length of preview is cut down, he feels the strain mounting, until he passes the threshold beyond which control is lost. Thereafter, being always late, he is always wrong. His performance becomes worse than random, unless the windings of the track are sufficiently regular for memory to supply the basis of prediction.[8]

Thus the designer of control mechanisms has two main problems. First, he has to elicit what is conveniently called a mis-match signal; that is, a signal which announces the discrepancy between what is and what ought to be. This norm, which sets the control, may be a goal to be sought, a course to be held, a state or a relationship to be maintained – anything, so long as deviations from it can be noted and (preferably) measured. Secondly, the signal must set off a process which will select and initiate an apt response. Each of the two problems may raise a multitude of difficulties and either may prove insoluble. The same principles apply to the control of a business enterprise and of the processes within it; but, when we apply the analysis to the control of business, it seems that the conditions in which control is possible are exceptional.

The manager has a battery of statistics to describe periodically the situation in regard to production, costs, deliveries, stocks, orders, cash balances and so on. These refer to situations in the past, being days, weeks or months in arrear. Generally speaking, these indices deal better with money than materials, with materials than with men, with external relations than with internal relations. For some important aspects of process there are as yet no adequate indices – for example, for morale. I think it will always be easier to interpret a change in the rate of capital turnover than in the rate of labour turnover.

Again, the value of these indices depends on our being able to compare them with what should have been on the date from which they speak; and here we have to rely on estimates of varying degrees of reliability. Modern techniques of control by budget and forecast all aim at supplying reliable indices of what ought to be for comparison with what is, so that the manager may be able more regularly to check whether the undertaking is doing what it is trying to do. In practice such estimates vary greatly in value.

Furthermore, at any given moment decisions are being taken, the results of which cannot yet be known. The span between the taking of a decision and the comparison of its actual with its intended result ranges from seconds to years; and the longer it is, the more likely it becomes that no comparison will ever be possible, since so many other variables will have contributed to affect the result. An interesting recent study suggests that this time span is the index by which we measure the weight of other people's responsibilities and our own.[9]

Again, the information which is derived from the mis-match signal in business seldom contains so much guidance as the helmsman receives from his compass. The automatic pilot can derive from observing the swing of the ship.s head all the information needed to correct it. The business manager may derive only the information that all is not well. When he sees that forecasts of production, orders, deliveries are not being fulfilled, he is put on enquiry but not necessarily given guidance. Still less is he guided where the frustrated expectation is in the field of human relations. His policy has not had the expected effect; should he continue it or intensify it or reverse it? The information does not tell him, until he has interpreted it by rules derived from elsewhere. It is not even a red light; for his policy may be right and his error may lie simply in his forecast of when it would show its effect.

A mere red light may be useful. There are situations in which it is sufficient that the agent shall run through its entire repertory of action, even at random, until an effective response is found. Machines have been made which work this way[10] and the process is not unknown in board-rooms, where it is signalled by the sinister phrase – 'We must do *something*'. But generally speaking, life at the higher levels of human organization moves too fast to admit of random action. The control must either contain or be capable of evolving rules which can guide it in selecting the appropriate response – if there is an appropriate response – which, of course, is not to be assumed.

It is time to supplement the idea of positive control by exploring negative control. Negative control could be illustrated by any of those devices which operate to prevent some critical limit being passed. Controls of boiler pressure and process temperature are obvious examples. The control is designed to sense when the assembly is approaching the danger point; before this is reached, it remains inactive. A simple example is supplied by a clockwork toy, which, when set to run on a table top, rushes about in all directions without falling over the edge. An antenna senses the edge when it is within reach and gives a twist to the direction. Since the goal is negative, any course which leads away from danger is as good as any other.

Negative control reminds us that every system works within limits which cannot be passed without disaster. Some conditions must be preserved if the assembly is to hold together; beyond them, the machine will break, the animal will die, the boat will capsize, the organization will break up, the business will go bankrupt. These changes are usually sudden, irreversible and complete; and when they threaten, the most cherished goals may have to be laid aside in order to escape them. Thus all positive goal-seeking, with the positive control which it involves, takes place within the framework of negative control, which ensures the continuance of the system.

When, in a tracking test, the track is narrow, it can be regarded equally well as a goal to be held or as two limits to be avoided; in other words, there is no difference between positive and negative control. But where the track is broad, the subject, whilst keeping within them, can choose a variety of courses. Having set himself a course, such as the central line, he can keep it by positive control; and only when he deviates wildly will he be conscious that limits not set by him confine his choices within a band of negative control. The analogy helps to make clear the relation between our self-chosen goals and those which the situation imposes on us.

So far I have talked as if the manager, at whatever level, were in charge of an integrated unit and were concerned only to regulate its interaction with the world outside, its *external* relations. But that is far from being the case. A business corporation is not an organism; nor at the other extreme is it a mere crowd. It is a highly structured society of a very peculiar kind. We are likely to make less serious mistakes if we regard it an as association of people than if we regard it as an imperfect entity.

At every level in a business organization we find positive and negative controls which are neither set by management nor under management's control. Each shop, each assembly line, each office has its own stabilities to guard and its own goals to pursue. It has them, it must have them and it should have them, if it is to be more than a crowd.

People sometimes liken a business corporation to an association of people with a common purpose, together achieving what all desire and none can achieve alone. This seems to me unrealistic. The forces which drive and regulate a great undertaking are legion and most diverse – individual need and ambition, the pleasures and frustrations of group activities as such, departmental habits and rivalries, professional standards and who knows what besides. The ultimate product and the ultimate profit are in a sense the by-products of thousands of diverse, individual strivings.[11]

Until recently, business management was unduly absorbed in external relations. This was natural; business corporations are formed to do business. Moreover, it is the curse of such cerebral creatures as we are to concentrate on external relations. It is a welcome development that management today should be looking inward. What it learns will not only make for efficiency in its outward relations. It will also enlighten us on what we most need to know.

The designer of control mechanisms produces machines which select the right responses in circumstances which used to require human judgment. They thus raise the question how much of the field of human choice can be explained in terms of control. What I have said already shows that there are three separate questions.

The evolution of organic forms has shown a widening in the field of choice in at least the three dimensions which I mentioned earlier. This widening of possibilities in the field of outer relationships has been largely due to the development of internal relationships. The same development is taking place in human institutions.

Whether at a given moment a particular organism is able to exercise any degree of choice is of course another matter. A man running in a race is exercising a choice, which deliberately excluded a host of alternatives. The same man with a bull after him has no choice but to run. Similarly, when a company, however large, is in the hands of its bankers, its directors have no choice but to do as the bank says – or rather, they have no choice consistent with continuing to function. When they meet to decide how to use super-abundant resources, they have a wide range of choice. What they choose will no doubt be determined by the system at the time but it will be determined by the state of the directors' heads rather than by the state of the company's bank balance.

This state of affairs is what I understand by having the initiative. It is created, preserved and lost largely by the way in which it is exercised. So long as it takes us all our time to keep alive, we have no choice of what to do with our lives. So long as it takes a company all its time to keep solvent, it has no choice of how it will develop. But as we learn to keep our systems – including ourselves – within their critical limits without undue effort, wider opportunities open within which we can set new goals and, to pursue them, build up self-maintaining activities of a higher order. The unskilled skater is wholly absorbed in keeping his balance; that is, in redressing the oscillations which his own efforts produce. The skilled skater has reduced his continuous balance-seeking to the level of unconscious adjustment; and in consequence he is free to skate as he pleases, that is to choose among an ever wider range of the things which are possible to men on skates. The analogy seems to me to hold for organisms and organizations at all levels. The range of their possible responses is limited; and within this limitation another narrower one is set by their situation, which itself is to some extent the result of their own conscious or unconscious choosing.

The question how, within these limitations, a particular choice is made is again another matter. Here, I think, the analysis of control can help us.

So far as I understand the exponents of cybernetics, there are only three theoretical limits to the ability of a control to find a response which will maintain any given state or course, if there is such a response within the assembly's repertory. These conditions are that past experience must be sufficiently regular to provide a guide for the future;[12] that the time taken to select the response and make it effective must not exceed the time within which the response is demanded; and that there must be criteria of success.

Within these limits there is room for great refinement. Thus, the simplest control mechanisms have the right responses built into them, each foreseen and set to be elicited by its appropriate signal. Such, for example, is the automatic pilot. Where this is impossible, we can build into the assembly rules for selecting the right response. Such, for example, would be a chess-playing machine. Finally, it is possible, at all events in theory, to build machines which will evolve their own rules in the light of their own experience.[13] Such, in embryo, are those automatic telephone exchanges which learn to make more quickly the connections which they have often made before.

These principles apply equally to the decisions of men and societies. Within the field which they cover, choice can be understood in terms of control and the analysis of control helps us to understand and improve our choosing. But the three limitations which I have mentioned exclude a large area within which we do in fact have to make choices. In business, as we have seen, the conditions of control are seldom fully present. We have to make assumptions about what is or what ought to be or both. Having made the assumptions, we have a choice of responses. Still more important, we can usually revise our goals and thus alter the datum from which our controls are derived; and we continually do so, partly to evade difficulties in pursuing them and partly to reconcile them with other goals which we are pursuing at the same time. This variety of choices makes up the continuous process of decision.

This process cannot, so far as I can see, be wholly explained in terms of control; but analysis in terms of control makes clearer the fields which remain to be explained. We have to explain how we set and change those positive and negative norms which control us; how we decide, when conditions of control are not present; and how we resolve the conflicts which arise, when these controls are at war. The model which I have presented so far does not help us with these problems, but I believe it has much more to teach us.

Meantime we can profit by its more obvious usefulness. It is useful to regard an organization as a tissue of feedback channels, to design it with this in mind and to interpret its achievements and failures in adaptivity in terms of the basic mechanisms of control, so far as these suffice. Most important, perhaps, it is useful to remember that the units of which it is composed are themselves highly complex organizations, possessing wide freedom of choice and governed by their own controls. Inconvenient as this may sometimes be, we should, I think, be unwise to change it, even if we could; for at the best it makes possible a combination of coherence and adaptability which would otherwise be far beyond our reach, whilst at the worst it prevents our organizations from becoming our masters and hence enables us continually to make them anew.

In this exploration I have been so rash as to speculate up to and beyond the boundary of my understanding. My only justification lies in a phrase with which I once heard a distinguished scientist end a highly technical address about the effect of drugs on the nervous system. He concluded – 'It is better to wonder than to explain.' He did not mean that we must ultimately bow before the unknowable, though that of course is true. Rather, he described perfectly the proper attitude for the scientist as he sits on the frontier of knowledge and looks out into the still unknown. We can explain only in terms of familiar concepts; but those concepts were once new and they were won by men who were not satisfied with any current explanations and who therefore wondered and went on wondering.

The engineer often becomes a manager but he should always remain a scientist. As a manager he will have little time to wonder; but as a scientist he has a duty to wonder. And if he finds a few moments to wonder now and then, he will be a better manager of men.

NOTES AND REFERENCES

[1] For a recent statement of this view I am indebted to Bertalanffy, L. von, *Problems of Life*. (1952) London: Watts and Co.

[2] This point is elaborated by Ruyer, R., *Néo-Finalisme*. (1952) Paris: Presses Universitaires de France, p. 89.

[3] Since these words were written, biologists believe that they have identified the structure which carries the genetic code. This astonishing achievement still falls short of breaking the code.

[4] Weizsäcker, C. F. von, *The History of Nature*. (1951) London: Routledge and Kegan Paul, p. 94.

[5] Cannon, W. B., *The Wisdom of the Body*. (1939) London: Routledge. Cannon and many others since have described the homeostatic processes of the body. The directiveness of organic behaviour as an observed phenomenon, irrespective of the rival theories which have been built on it, has been described by Russell, E. S., in *The Directiveness of Organic Activities* (1945. Cambridge University Press); and the justification for accepting this provisionally as an organic law which is not at present to be further resolved has been cogently stated by Dingle, H., in *The Scientific Adventure*. (1952) London: Pitman, pp. 249 and 250.

[6] Space does not permit me to explore these modes of interaction adequately here. I distinguish competition from conflict, though I am aware that many regard it as merely a form of conflict. Trees in a wood mututally intensify their propensity to grow taller and mutually restrain their tendency to grow laterally. It seems to me that two forms of interaction which have such markedly different effects deserve different names. The fact that some, defeated in the race for light and air, wither and die, merely shows that the competitive situation may become conflictual. The analysis of co-operation would unduly expand the limits of a note.

[7] The question is, of course, debatable. Space does not permit me to attempt a justification of the view here expressed. Much of the evidence is reviewed in the proceedings of a conference held at the University of Chicago in 1942 and edited by Dr Robert Redfield, c.f. particularly the paper on higher levels of integration by Dr R. W. Gerard, who would seem to hold a view different from that which is here expressed. (Redfield, R., editor, 'Levels of Integration in Biological and Social Systems', Vol. VIII of *Biological Symposia*. (1942) Lancaster, Pennsylvania: The Jacques Cattell Press.)

[8] c.f. Poulton, E. C., 'Anticipation in Open and Closed Sensori-motor Skills'.

(1950) Medical Research Council Applied Psychology Research Unit Report No. 138.

[9] c.f. Jacques, E., *Measurement of Responsibility*. (1956) London: Tavistock Publications, pp. 52–60.

[10] Such is the homeostat described by Ashby, Ross W., in *Design for a Brain*. (2nd ed. 1960) London: Chapman and Hall.

[11] This apparent paradox is more fully treated by Simon, H. A., in *Administrative Behaviour*. (2nd ed. 1959) New York: Macmillan, pp. 17 and 18.

[12] The possibility, referred to above, that a random running through of the repertory of responses will in time provide the right one is no exception to this statement; for it assumes that the situation will remain regular at least throughout the period of search and for sufficiently long thereafter to enable the response to be effectively used.

[13] These possibilities are analysed in a paper to which I am indebted in many ways by Mackay, D. M., 'Towards an Information-Flow Model of Human Behaviour', *British Journal of Psychology*. (1956) p. 33.

CHAPTER EIGHT

The Concept of 'Incentive'*

THE TWENTY-THREE million men and women who are earning their livings in Britain today are infinitely diverse individuals; the work they do and the situations in which they do it are varied past telling; and the motives which move them are unguessably complex. Is it useful to bundle together these millions of diversities under such abstract labels as 'labour' and 'incentives'? Can anything useful be said at such a level of generality? I think it can; but only if we keep in mind how varied are the human realities which underlie them. I begin, then, by suggesting three dimensions along which we may classify the infinite variety of jobs which together provide us with the goods and services we use and with our main individual titles to share in them.

The customary distinction between manual work on the one hand and clerical and administrative work on the other has, I believe, none but historical significance. The division into 'industrial' and 'non-industrial' work is even more artificial. The sooner we grow out of both, the better. The first dimension which I would offer is based simply on the amount of physical energy which the work demands. At one end of the scale are the jobs which are done seated, whether at a typewriter, a comptometer, a chocolate-wrapping machine, a drawing-board, or a managing director's desk. At the other extreme are those jobs, still numerous, in which human muscles are employed as prime movers. These include much of mining and quarrying, of iron and steel industry, of building and agriculture, as well as general labouring and some unexpected trades like the surviving non-mechanized bakeries. They might be described not as manual but as 'dorsal' jobs. Between these two extremes stretch in continuous gradation jobs of varying physical

*Originally published under the title *Incentives of Labour*.

activity, among which the travelling salesman may be found to rank higher than many manual workers. The housewife, being unpaid, does not challenge us to classify her. I suspect that on this scale she usually ranks higher than her husband.

I do not suggest for a moment that work is unacceptable in proportion to the amount of physical labour involved. On the contrary, young people usually take more willingly to active work than to an office stool. The difference is none the less important, I believe, from the point of view of motivation. Experiment has shown that the natural pace for physical work is irregular, fluctuating frequently and widely. No similar work has been done, so far as I know, on mental work but it may well be that its rhythms, if it has them, are at a much slower tempo. Moreover, though the physiological nature of fatigue and its effect on performance are still imperfectly understood, it seems to me to be a fact of observation that mental work, however exacting, can be maintained – and pleasurably maintained – at maximum speed for much longer than heavy physical labour.

The dimension which I have been discussing I will call 'the degree of physical involvement'. I turn now to my second, which might be called 'the degree of mental involvement'. Jobs range along this dimension from those which require only the most automatic movement of the hand to those involving extremes of concentration, initiative, judgment, originality, or responsibility. The bearing of these differences on motivation are even more obscure; for mental fatigue is not measurable, whilst mental stress is a most imprecise concept. There is no doubt, however, that these differences affect motivation and further that their effect varies greatly with the individual. Monotony is as great a stress to one man as responsibility is to another. Moreover in this, as in other respects, the individual is not a constant. What he will like and what he will stand vary with his age, his training and experience, his personal circumstances and his personal development, as well as with his relations in the social situation of the work-place.

One other dimension must be included. For nearly everyone the first day's work is a start on a road which offers some hope of advancement to different work, higher status and more money. Again, for virtually everyone there comes a day when this prospect is closed, when the future holds only the expectation of repeating the present. But the point at which the prospect of progress thus ceases to operate may come very early or very late. Thus, for careers for which apprentice-ship is a necessary entry, the door may close at sixteen. The late Mr Ernest Bevin once observed, 'It's a funny country. A fitter's mate can become Prime Minister but he can't become a fitter.' I do not know how far this limitation still obtains. The extension of part-time educa-tion, especially in engineering in conjunction with the various forms of national certificate, combined with the increasing practice of release with pay has multiplied the opportunities of access to careers which need an educational qualification. From nearly every position today some ladder leads upwards; but there is an age limit and usually an early one, above which it becomes first difficult and soon impossible to get a foot on these ladders. Most people in industry reach their ceil-ing by thirty. Those who get their foot on the ladder of managmeent usually reach their ceiling between thirty and the fifties. Few, save judges, 'progress' in their career beyond that age.

I am not drawing attention to something which seems to me to be either remediable or regrettable. I am merely pointing out that at any given moment only a minority of the people engaged in earning their livings are or can be validly motivated by the desire to 'progress' in their careers. I will call this dimension 'the degree of career involve-ment'.

So far I have avoided using the word 'incentives'. It savours of the 'kick and carrot' mentality of the nineteenth century and has fallen into disrepute. It suggests that, at least in their economic behaviour, men are chiefly concerned to pursue individual goals and to avoid in-dividual threats and it carries the further connotation that these goals and threats are economic.

This fallacious psychology has indeed been changed out of all recog-nition in the last fifty years. The motivations of men remain obscure; but laymen as well as scientists are now aware of the main defects of the old view. First, the behaviour of men is not to be explained wholly as the seeking of goals and the avoidance of threats. Activity is satisfying or dissatisfying in its own right, as experience, apart from the ends it serves. Further, these satisfactions, whether direct or indirect, are socially conditioned; the individual is a social animal, at work no less than at home. Indeed, industry is a highly structured society, in which the roles we play are more inter-related and more closely defined than in most other social situations. Finally, in so far as we seek goals and avoid threats, they are more fundamental than money will explain. We seek success and security in devious ways. Money, as a means, as an end, and as a symbol is only one of many constituents in the net of our hopes and fears.

This re-valuation of industrial society has worked a profound change. On the one hand it has made visible a number of situations which are relevant to the way men work. On the other hand, it has shown that the variables which management can influence or control for good and ill are far more numerous than it imagined. Both merit analysis.

Thus, among work situations, we can distinguish solitary jobs from jobs which are done in teams. Observation has shown that men working alone behave in some respects differently from men working in teams. It has not shown that for all men in all situations the one always yields better results than the other; but it has shown that the degree of team involvement is relevant to the way men work.

We can also distinguish work situations according to the degree to which the worker identifies himself with the success of the operation in which he is engaged. We may call this job involvement; and we must distinguish it from team involvement, for work teams may and often do achieve their highest significance for their members in pursuing goals which are remote from the job – their own security, for example, or their advance in prestige. Within the category of job involvement we must note further that the job with which the worker becomes involved may be seen by him as his own immediate product or as the product of his department or of the whole undertaking; and the level with which he thus identifies himself may be highly important in the total pattern of motivation.

The same question of levels complicates the analysis of team involvement. How remote an interest or a loyalty can a man compass? What combination of loyalties or interests can he entertain without undue conflict? We know too little of the factors which govern the answers to such questions but we see around us plenty of examples to show how important they are. The Royal Navy, for example, focuses loyalty on the ship and on the Service and seems to be highly successful in combining the two. It would, however, be easy to give examples in which concentric or interlocking loyalties yield endless tension and confusion.

We may also include among the main classifications of work situations the quality of those transmitted attitudes which establish the climate of every society. Working groups are linked with their past and their transmitted culture powerfully determines the motivations which shall operate within them. The problems involved in changing an evil heritage of this kind are among the most important and intractable of management and, despite valuable research, are also among the most obscure.

I have spent some time on a bare and partial summary of the varieties of job and of work situation. There remains another critical variable. Men themselves vary and their variations are at least as obscure as those I have examined hitherto. A great deal of work has been done in devising tests for human skills and in classifying more general traits of character and temperament. The results do not yet give management tools adequate to the task of fitting men to jobs and jobs to men; but at least they have made us conscious that individual differences are real and that they matter. The motivations of one man are not necessarily those of another.

Such, I suggest, are the main variables in the industrial scene. On their interaction depends the effectiveness with which men combine to earn their collective and individual livings in the highly complex and artificial world we live in.

We can now state more clearly the question which underlies the title to this paper. What are the factors which encourage men to respond or which discourage men from responding to the demands which work makes on them? And what can management do to foster the one and dispel the other? The answers will vary with the job, the man, and the situation; and in each case individual and social, positive and negative motivations will be found differently combined. In the space which remains to me I will comment on what seem to me to be the most important issues in the main fields which management can influence.

Reward remains a profoundly important factor in motivation. It largely determines whether we work at all – as distinct from all the attractive alternatives which we might otherwise pursue – and, to an important, though lesser degree, the work we choose to do. In some work it plays a part in determining how much we do. On the other hand, it has, I think, little direct influence on how well we work, still less on how co-operatively we work. Its main effect in Britain today is, I am convinced, negative. Discontent with reward is probably the most important factor in discouraging us from responding to the demands of work today.

Since I am confining myself to matters on which the individual management has some initiative and therefore some responsibility, I have nothing to say about the strange and most unsatisfactory process by which the absolute level of reward is fixed. Nothing could be more disruptive of our responses to the demands of work than the constant pursuit of prices by wages; but wage and price policy are not within the scope of this paper.

On the other hand, the fixing of one level in relation to another – the vexed problem of differentials – is clearly within its field. The situation here is highly unsatisfactory for employer and employee alike. We lack any agreed and objective measure of the relative value of different jobs and at least three rival and disparate measures compete for predominance. Tradition and vested interest entrench the *status quo*. Work study slowly erodes these defences with its more rational though still subjective measurements. And now and then both are abruptly displaced by the impact of supply and demand. First one and then another role becomes unexpectedly critical, because of an absolute lack of those willing to accept it, be they science teachers or loco-drivers, nurses or coal-miners. The need is met by a revaluation of the unfilled role; and the repercussions set going a cycle precisely calculated to defeat the adjustment which has been made. The object of the exercise, be it the objective one of filling the posts or the subjective one of ensuring contentment regresses infinitely.

The importance of such difficulties varies greatly from one occupation to another; I believe it to be related almost entirely to the ratio which wages and salaries bear to total costs. In those happy occupations where this ratio is low, reward is usually a major positive factor in building up satisfaction with work and confidence in the employer. Where the ratio is high, problems of wage-fixing tend to be most acute and the disincentives associated with them are maximal. In this respect public, non-profit-making bodies are often worse placed than private undertakings, since they are less certain what they can and cannot afford. Moreover they are further handicapped by never feeling rich.

The way wage and salary rates are settled, no less than their absolute and relative level, powerfully affects the attitude of the employee to the undertaking and thus bears indirectly on his motivation; for the settlement of a rate between employer and employee is an occasion on which confidence is either won or lost. One way or the other, it makes the employer real. It is significant, then, that the level at which wage rates are fixed is changing. There are still places where the rate for each new job is fixed direct between manager and workman. In some of these places it is a main source of trouble; in others a mainspring of confidence. In contrast to both, British industry moves increasingly towards a rigid structure of few grades, nationally fixed. It is of no small moment for work motivation that this cuts out, both for good and for ill, a critical contact between management and worker.

Of real, though in my view of less importance is the way in which wages are calculated. This may vary vastly. Some men are paid simply on a piece rate; others on a time rate with a bonus variously related to results; others on a simple time rate. Where payment is related to result, it may be geared to the achievement of the individual or of a team, large or small, of which he is part or of the whole undertaking. Where it is related to time, it may be based on the hour, the day, the week, the month or the year; and it may or may not be additional to over-time, variously calculated. Examples could be found to illustrate each of these variations working well – and working ill.

Nothing that we know of human nature, nothing that we observe in human behaviour gives us any firm ground for thinking that any of these patterns is the best for all situations or for any situation. There is evidence to stress the obvious fact that, where payment is based on the results of a team, the body chosen should be one which actually feels and behaves as a team, not merely one which is supposed to do so. Further, there is some evidence that piece work has more justification, both psychological and physiological, for 'dorsal' work than for other kinds. Thus, it can be used – though it very seldom is used – to enable the worker to set his own pace. Generally speaking, however, I see no reason to hope that research and experiment will reveal a 'best' way. The adaptations of life are singularly various. And, where in any sit-uation there proves to be a 'best', its pre-eminence will, I think, be found to derive, not from some unchanging characteristics of the human psyche but from the particular situation, with all its load of history.

Thus, the various methods of payment have become linked with different levels of prestige and status and these links persist, even though the differences which created them are passing. For example, the ancient distinction between 'hands' and 'staff' excluded the hourly-paid and daily-paid workers both from the privileges and from the responsibil-ities of 'belonging'. The privileges are being added piecemeal by guar-anteed weeks, pension schemes, and so on, so that the actual situation of the two classes in regard to security grows ever more similar; but the old schism remains and still deeply affects the motivations of the two.

I turn next to promotion. The procedure by which people are pre-pared and selected for higher posts is of lively concern, not only to the minority who aspire to promotion but also to the majority who do not. Thus it may powerfully affect the responses of both groups. The aim of any promotion policy must be to ensure that for every vacancy, as it occurs, there shall be enough, but not too many candidates, eager for the job and qualified to do it by character, temperament, experience, and training. If such a policy is to pull its full weight on the right side in the complex of influences which bear on motivation, it must be understood and its working approved and trusted. In industries where management inherits the suspicion of nepotism or victimization, great and prolonged efforts may be needed to restore the position and these may be of high importance from the point of view of work motivation.

I have discussed pay and promotion first, because they most closely resemble individual incentives. Yet even this brief analysis has shown that they are at least as important in their impact on the attitude of employees to the undertaking and thus on the response of those employees to its demands on them. I will now consider this aspect of motivation further.

A man's response to the demands of work depends very much on his attitude to the employer, to the undertaking, and to the job. These three are significantly different and I think I have stated them in inverse order of importance. What matters most is attitude to the job and to that part of the undertaking and its management which are within the direct experience of the worker. The more remote parts of the undertaking, the higher ranks of management, make progressively less impact on him for good or ill. Indirectly the policy and control of top management may be decisive in maintaining a favourable climate in his immediate environment but its hand is and should be largely unseen. Top management should in this regard be self-effacing. Pyramids should be built from the bottom.

In modern management many techniques are directly concerned with building the employee's sense of belonging. Among these are industrial consultation, the giving of financial and other information about the firm, suggestion schemes, 'cross-sectional' schools and conferences. I believe these techniques to be of great value; but in large undertakings they raise acutely the question of the level at which the sense of belonging should be focused. I regard this as one of the major unsettled questions in the field of motivation. The evidence goes to show that 'belonging' must start in the work-place. It may with advantage extend upwards as far as may be, so as to give some feeling of identification with any level from which a disturbing – or even an encouraging – impact may be felt; but the lowest levels are the most important, both because they affect the individual's behaviour most directly and because it is on them that the higher levels depend.

At the working level all these involvements tend to be resolved into 'team involvement'; that is, into the sense of belonging to a working group. Most of the demands of the work express themselves as the demands – or, more commonly, the unspoken expectations – of work-mates, including the representatives of management in charge of the group. I have already pointed out that team involvement and job involvement are not necessarily the same. It is obviously important that they should be the same; for it is largely through the mutual responses of men to men in the working situation that the needs of the job can be translated into practice. Over these inter-personal relations management has less direct influence but it impinges on them in at least two important ways – first, through its designing of the teams themselves and, secondly, through its training and appointment of the team's leaders.

A well-known study in the coal industry analyses the social effect of introducing a new technical process of coal-getting. Briefly, a series of operations, once performed by one man and his mate, was divided between three teams, working on successive shifts. The work of each team depended on the previous team completing its work thoroughly and to time.

Thus, the design of the work required the three teams to feel and act as one, although they never met. There were, indeed, factors which made it hard even for any one of the teams to act as such. These difficulties were not present to the minds of those who introduced the new technique. Regarding the problem as a technical one, it did not occur to them that success would depend also on social responses, which had not been needed before and which would not be naturally or easily evoked. Similar problems exist elsewhere, though today they are less likely to be overlooked. The design of team work needs to take account of psychological limitations which are as yet very imperfectly known.

Probably the greatest opportunity which management possesses to evoke and maintain from all its employees the responses which the work requires is through its power to select, train and support its own representatives and especially its foremen and managers, who form part of the actual work team at the work-place. They also form part of another team, more dispersed but not less important – the management team. In any large organization the working of the management team must be the prime concern of top management. The 'incentives of management' – or as we have translated our title, the factors which make management at all levels respond as they need to do to the demands of their particular work – are crucial to the 'incentives of labour'.

The Impact of Automation*

BY AUTOMATION I understand primarily the progressive replacement of men by machines in the field of *control*.

Mechanization first lent men *energy*, enabling them to use human skill on tasks beyond human muscles. Next, it began to take over their *skills*, progressively reducing the majority of manual workers to machine minders and concentrating human skills in the functions of machine designing and machine setting.

The new developments, as I understand it, go much further, promising to replace the machine minder, the shop supervisor, even part of the functions of the works manager by machines and assemblies of machines which control themselves. Somewhere, no doubt, there will be a point beyond which the assembly can only call for help, signalling some failure or defect which it cannot itself correct; so somewhere there will still be a man, ready to be alerted by a distress signal on an instrument panel; but in theory this point may be almost infinitely remote. We had better assume that there are no instructions too complex to be given to a machine, provided they relate to activities within its compass which can be specified; or which can be arrived at by rules which can be specified; or by rules which can be learned in specified ways; or even . . . But perhaps I have gone far enough to satisfy the automation enthusiast that I do not underrate the sweep of his horizons.

These techniques go much further than the control of machines and mechanical assemblies or even the control of physical processes, such as the phasing of supply of materials and components to the places and at the rates required. They extend also to the collection, storage and

*An address given in September 1963 in Toronto at a conference on automation and social change, organized by the Government of Ontario.

processing of all data which can be digitally coded or represented by any form of analogue. They are therefore capable of taking over all or nearly all processes of calculation now done by men, from the preparation of a weekly pay sheet to the calculation of joint life annuity rates from the latest mortality tables; and of doing many calculations previously impracticable through the sheer labour involved, like some of the calculations involved in rocketry; even of imitating some mental processes which we cannot reduce to calculation like the recognition of form.

Processing is a wide word. It covers all specifiable operations which present or future computers can be set to do; and this includes many of the constituents of human decision and human judgment. How many we do not know, because we do not know how far our present inability to specify our own mental processes is due merely to our ignorance and how far it is due to peculiarities of the processes themselves. Automation, then, may be able to take over not only most of our controlling and calculating activities but also an uncertain proportion of what seem our most human discretions.

So when we try to discern the impact of automation on society, we should not regard it simply as a further stage of that familiar process which we know as industrialization; or assume that its impact on us will be the same as the impact of earlier stages or that we shall be able to deal with it as we dealt with them. I believe we shall not; and this is only partly due to the peculiarities of automation to which I have referred. It is due also to the stage of industrialization which we have already reached. So we must, I think, first form some view of the state of Western industrial societies in their present stage of industrialization, before we try to forecast the impact of this further and novel instalment. (Let me apologize in advance for the inaccuracies of which I am bound to be guilty in speaking of so wide a generalization as 'Western industrial societies' from a knowledge, primarily, of my own alone. I can find no other way of handling the subject, without too many tiresome qualifications.)

The Impact of Automation

It is extremely difficult to talk about anything so complex as society without first reducing it to manageable order and I must spend a few minutes in describing what seems to me the simplest order which will serve our purpose. I will ask you to conceive your society in terms of three sets of variables. There is first what I might call the physical state of the nation, which could be described in terms of things measurable and observable, such as population, capital equipment, production, income levels, health, employment, housing, undeveloped land, power, water and so on. All these are facts which would be as they might be, whether anyone noticed them or not; but their actual state is as it is, because people do notice them and respond to them and do things about them; and all this depends on another state of the system, which I will call the cultural state. This consists of the concepts and values in people's heads, their idea of the world they live in, of what is desirable and what unacceptable and what matters most. It is, in brief, the way they appreciate their situation and it is this, so far as it is shared, which gives coherence to a society.

This cultural state contains ideas not only of how things are but of how they ought to be. It contains, for example, the novel idea that in a modern industrialized society, a rising standard of living should co-exist with full employment. Differences between the way things seem to be going and the way we think they ought to be going are of great importance, because these disparities are the signals which guide policy and call for action. They are to a social system what the mis-match signals of the engineer are to a self-regulating system in industry.

But before we can form an idea of what a society will actually do in response to such signals, we have to look at yet another state of the nation, which I will call the institutional state. This includes the society's institutions of government and business and law and its social institutions, like the family and the ways in which these are set to act. These are the means through which a society copes with its problems and they also limit what it can do. They even affect what it will notice.

The factors which make up all three states, the physical, the cultural and the institutional, are changing all the time and changes in any set affect the other two, which is why it is so hard to talk or think clearly about impacts on society. But without too much simplification we can say that these mis-match signals which make 'impacts' on us may arise because the actual course of events, as we perceive it, begins to depart from what we regard as acceptable or because our ideas of what is acceptable begin to change, so that we feel impelled to alter what we were formerly ready to accept – or, of course, through the operation of both. Unemployment, for example, may rise 'unacceptably' according to current standards; or we may change our ideas of the level of unemployment which we should accept.

And this brings me to what I believe to be the root of the dilemma, a dilemma which exists already, apart from automation. In developed Western states both the physical and the cultural state of the nation have changed and are changing. We expect our societies to meet complex and increasing demands for affluence, security, status and ease; and to meet them not just on the whole and over the years but for the great majority of us and every year. Most of these expectations are novel; our institutions were not designed to meet them. What economist or business man a century ago, what politician, what voter could have conceived a situation in which governments might fall if vacant jobs and idle men failed to balance within a margin of less than five per cent? We do not know what changes in our institutions or in our other expectations would be needed to enable these demands to be met or whether they can be met at all. And that is why the growth of automation at this stage is likely, in my view, to have unusually violent repercussions.

Consider first the separate, though related questions of unemployment and leisure. Every year a large number of young people become available for employment. Apart from immigration and emigration, this number is virtually fixed by birth rates and mortality rates over several previous years. The capacities of these people, in so far as it depends on their genetic heritage and on their education and training up to maturity, are also by that time 'given'. Their numbers are greater than the vacancies caused by death and retirement. Yet we expect them all to find places as producers and we have no other means of giving them status either as consumers or as members of society. The increase both in the numbers of producers and in productivity is supposed to be absorbed 'automatically' by more consumers, a higher rate of consumption and increased leisure.

I am not an economist but I see no reason why this equation should hold indefinitely and still less why it should hold 'automatically'. It would hold, even in theory, only if consumption were indefinitely expansible and leisure infinitely divisible; and it would hold automatically only if the system included automatic regulators for distributing both purchasing power and leisure. None of these conditions exists and the history of our institutional development, no less, I believe, in North America than in Europe, has been largely the history of successive attempts to create such regulators. So this is perhaps the place to take a glance at this aspect of the institutional state of the nation.

For two centuries the Western world has been exploring first the possibilities and then the limitations of the greatest automatic regulator of human affairs ever devised by man. This is a free market in goods, services, labour, money and ideas and free access to those markets for all. This is far more than a prescription for economic expansion. Its early enthusiasts believed that it would ensure indefinitely, peaceful change in the direction of the self-defined well-being of each and all. This proved, unhappily, too much to expect of it and the last century has seen its weaknesses patched by successive corrections, similar in kind in every country concerned.

The system first proved inadequate to distribute the purchasing power required fully to meet its own needs. This defect was patched, partly be re-distributing income through differential taxation and state benefits and partly by collective bargaining. It proved, further, inadequate to meet those demands that call for collective, rather than individual spending, the demand, for example, for roads, as distinct from automobiles; and this was patched by diverting ever more spending from the private to the public sector. It proved still more inadequate to meet those needs which are least readily supplied through a market at all, in particular those services like education, medical care and many welfare services, which are needed primarily by those least able to make their wants felt through a market; and this failure was exaggerated by the weakening of institutions like the family and the local community, through which they had once been met. These defects are now being patched by the effort to create, professionally and institutionally, all those supportive services which the social institutions of the country no longer supply.

Above all, this system proved inadequate to regulate its own growth; for example, to regulate the growth of cities, the distribution of land use and the patterns of communication. These defects were patched first by developing an increasing net of negative governmental powers, to curtail what was not deemed to be in the public interest; and then by an increasing number of public agencies, like the Hydro and the Seaway authorities, designed positively to do what needed to be done.

Alongside these institutional changes, there have been important cultural changes. The so-called 'private' institutions of business are expected and even expect themselves to accept responsibilities for the social implications of what they do, which would have scandalized the business men of even one generation before.

Thus there has emerged the familiar picture of the 'mixed economy' – familiar, that is to say, to us who live in it. It may be that to future ages or even to our contemporaries in other cultures it may seem like one of those evolutionary monstrosities which have exhausted all their possibilities of piecemeal adjustment and must now mutate or disappear.

One of the less encouraging aspects of the system is that, despite the existence of large areas of unsatisfied need, consumption is maintained partly by mammoth expenditure on unconsumable services like armaments and space research and partly by deliberately designed waste, commonly called 'built-in obsolescence'. But more serious, perhaps, is the current weakness of the system in distributing leisure. This is done, so far as it is done, in two ways. On the one hand, government, by a variety of constraints and inducements, increases the years which we spend in education and in retirement and thereby to some extent reduces the working population; though this has been more than offset since the war by the increase, officially encouraged, in the number of married women at work. On the other hand, the weekly hours per head actually worked falls, though slowly, through the demands of the employed. It is not surprising that the creation of leisure should be even more sluggish within the system than outside; for the system is set to maximize what can be sold and leisure cannot be sold. Moreover, since in our culture, itself largely the product of the system, status and success are closely geared to employment and income, demands for leisure are likely to be half-hearted.

You may find this report on the institutional state of the nation unduly dark and distorted. It may be so; but I believe that it stresses those aspects which we need to have in mind when we try to forecast the social impacts of automation. I am concerned with impacts, not with effects. I cannot predict what the effects will be, here or elsewhere; I believe that they are logically unpredictable, for they depend on the responses of men and institutions to events which have not yet happened and to the effects of their own responses. All I shall attempt is to explore some of the first impacts on societies constituted as I believe ours to be and to enquire what responses are likely to be open and at what cost.

I choose four impacts. Automation must increase, perhaps dramatically, the productivity of industry; and this dividend must be taken in increased consumption or in unemployment or in leisure – in fact, no doubt, in all three. Further, as I understand, automation is likely to operate selectively in a way not seen before. Hand operatives made idle by the spinning shafts and dangling belts of nineteenth century mills returned in time to produce more, though usually with less skill; but the men and women made idle by automation will not be needed to operate the machines which displace them. They will need greater or different skills to regain a place in the world of work. Further, they will include clerical and supervisory, as well as manual workers; workers not only in industry but in every branch of administration, and not least in government. Thirdly, automation will affect the organization and the thinking of all those organizations which adopt it – again, a far more comprehensive group than were affected by any previous impact of industrialization.

Finally, in so far as the dividend is taken in the form of leisure or unemployment – and some of it must, I think, take one or the other of these forms, it will have an impact on this 'leisured' sector of social life, the sector not structured by the demands of work, which might wholly change its character.

In considering these four impacts, we might usefully bear in mind one truth of fairly general application. When a society of any kind is called on to adapt to some change in the relation between its perceived situation and the standards by which it judges this to be acceptable – when, in other words, the stream of mis-match signals alert it to the need to do something other than it is already doing – it normally proceeds along the line of least resistance. First, it intensifies familiar responses; then it may devise others; it may even set up new institutions to give effect to them. Next it may be forced to modify its existing institutions to make room for the new, and to accept, at first only as a temporary measure, changes in its culture which these necessitate. Only in the last resort will it be driven to question the assumptions which create the problem, to ask whether the question which it is trying to answer is in fact the right question, to ask for example not just how to maintain full employment *and* rising productivity but whether either, let alone both is what ought to be at the top of our list of priorities. Yet this is the kind of question which most needs to be asked early. It is the question we ought to be asking now.

Consider then first the impact of rapid and prolonged increase in productivity, sufficient to upset unacceptably the precarious balance between available jobs and people available to do them.

If new responses are needed, what are available? The most obvious is some means of giving production away. It is indisputable that most of the world is short of the necessities of life and that even in prosperous societies real poverty still exists. Employment could be found for some time at least for all potential producers, even in prosperous countries, in creating surpluses for other people to consume – provided that those others were content to consume more than they produced and had some system, as we have not, for distributing unearned surpluses.

This situation is not new. Much of Britain's export surpluses in the nineteenth century were paid for out of the proceeds of British loans which were never repaid and many of which, as later economists would have seen, never had a chance of being repaid. Some U.S. surpluses since the war have been distributed more rationally and generously as 'aid'. Is this process capable of development on an entirely new scale? Is it likely to be? Should it be? I do not know. If it were developed, internally as well as externally on a scale to meet the need, it would have social as well as economic effects for it would change our institutions and our ideas about human rights and duties. Failing this, we have to consider the problem of absorbing this unused and unusable capacity in the form of leisure or unemployment. Before exploring this, let us look for a moment at the second of my chosen impacts, the selective nature of automation's impact on employment.

How serious this qualitative threat may be I do not know. Any man, however unskilled, is capable of discriminations which could be equalled, if at all, only by the most sophisticated and expensive bit of automation. One of the few industrial studies to be made by a psychiatrist[1] found no single job, however humble, in an entire factory, to which some element of discretion was not essential. A night watchman, dozing over a coke brazier by some road contractor's site, if he could still be found, might seem a nineteenth century relic; but the poor fellow, clinging to the margin of unskilled employment, can tell the difference between a cat upsetting a pile of bricks and a thief making off with the day shift's gear; and it would take a fabulously expensive piece of automation to do as much. The returning day shift, with their picks and shovels, will be more than a match for a mechanical digger, however automatically controlled, when it comes to uncovering a water main at the still uncertain point where it has burst. Examples could be multiplied. I have had a great respect for unskilled work since I saw supposedly unskilled men in British coal-mines handling free running trucks of coal, on dark gradients underground, in conditions in which I felt sure that many high-powered administrators of my acquaintance would have been rolled flat in an hour. It seems to me that there is a field, and an extensive field, in which men, even illiterate men, can compete with machines, whether as control mechanisms or as computers, for as far ahead as I can see.

The fact remains that many jobs, manual, clerical and supervisory will be taken over by machines in the next decade; and it is not to be assumed that the men and women so displaced can be retained for *any* work which will then be available, even in conditions of otherwise full employment. The social effects of this depend on how extensive and how rapid a development it proves to be and on this the economic prophets differ. I want at this stage to make only two comments on it. The first concerns the rate of change.

It is sometimes said that every technological change that comes is 'bound to come'; sometimes even that its rate of coming cannot be controlled. These defeatist observations are, I believe, false. Those who make them really mean either that to resist or seek to check such changes would be wrong, by some canon which they have accepted too deeply even to defend; or that its cost would be more than they would think worth paying – though exponents of the view seldom count the cost of *not* containing the rate of change. As Norbert Weiner has observed[2] – 'It is one of the paradoxes of the human race . . . that the people who control the fortunes of our community should at the same time be wildly radical in matters that concern our own change of our environment and rigidly conservative in the social matters that determine our adaptation to it.'

Of course the rate of change can be controlled; most regulation consists in phasing divergent rates of change. Only the 'id' cannot wait; and it is the ego's business to teach it manners. It is true that our present official regulators are ill adapted to regulate technological change in industry; but our official regulators are being forced to learn new tricks in this, as in other fields; and other powerful regulators could help them, if the will were there. Industry has some experience of delaying innovation until investment on the phase to be replaced has been recovered; and in the matter of changes affecting employment, trade union organization supplies a regulator happily more powerful today than that improvised by the Luddite workmen who broke up the new machinery in my native town of Nottingham one hundred and fifty years ago. The lesson which Canute taught his flattering courtiers from his encounter with the tide was to recognize independent variables. I do not doubt that that competent executive (who ruled my country at the age of twenty-three) would have given his counsellors an even sharper object lesson, if they had tried to persuade him that he could not control unwelcome tides of their own making.

My second comment concerns the future of those occupations and professions which cannot readily be automatized. Some simpler aspects of teaching may pass to teaching machines; but I hope that a day will not come when we are automatically nursed, or legally advised or even medically diagnosed though I know this last is technically a likely field of exploration. Will these occupations, some of them under-manned and under-esteemed today, grow in prestige and in quality through the automatizing of activities which today compete for their recruits? If this should occur, it would introduce a great and beneficent social change. Logically we might expect it. Surely, as the meeting of our simpler needs becomes more and more automatized, prestige should gravitate to those services which can be rendered to men only by men?

Logically it should; but psychologically I doubt whether it will. The reasons appear from a consideration of my third impact area, the effect of automation on the organization and thinking of industry and of all other activities which come to depend on it, especially the activities of government.

Mechanization has caused the progressive atrophy of jobs which cannot be mechanized. The market carries more and more mass-produced products – differing from each other less and less – but it becomes harder and harder to buy anything which is not mass-produced or to get any kind of individual service; harder, for instance, to get an erratic ballcock mended than to buy a new sink-unit. As automation spreads, will products which cannot be automated wilt in the same way? I fear that they will, not merely in face of economic competition from processes which automation has genuinely cheapened but from the prestige of the new technique. The spearhead of technological advance will be the automation of processes not automated before. That is where the brains, the enthusiasm and the money will be. Business is an adventure for those who conduct it, an investment only for the faceless, voiceless millions who finance it. The judgment 'this job needs a man', even the judgment 'this job doesn't need an automaton' may be only a business judgment to the financier but it will seem like a confession of failure to the development engineer. I have no doubt that industry will distort and narrow its function to no small degree to get the new techniques in.

This, however, seems to me a relatively slight danger, compared with the corresponding danger inherent in automating processes of data-handling and decision. In this field the new processes will of course have solid as well as specious merits. They will be quick and reliable within their limitations. They will carry the authority of calculation, as against mere opinion; what they produce will be not 'an answer' but 'the answer'. And they will not easily be combined in a process in which any single element cannot be specified. How great the temptation to specify the uncertain, to omit the doubtful, to simplify the problem sufficiently to get it on to the machine! And once it is there, who will discover or even remember the built-in limitation?

I am influenced by personal experience, even in this still unautomated world, of the power of the measurable to dwarf the non-measurable. I recall times when I have criticized some forecast or estimate for omitting some variable which must obviously be relevant to the result and have been answered – 'We couldn't include that; we couldn't put a value on it.' And if I objected – 'But by omitting it, you have valued it at zero; and you know that is the only value it *cannot* have.' The answer – given in the sad, patient voice which the professional keeps for the amateur – would be – 'No; we haven't valued it; we have only *omitted* it.' And then, triumphantly – 'Look, one of the footnotes says so.'

I fear the alluring possibilities of automating decision processes, first, because the decisions which lend themselves to be so treated are decisions about the best means to reach given ends, where the criteria by which means are judged best are given, like the 'ends', at the outset. I believe that no important decisions are of this type and that those which appear to be so usually conceal more important questions which ought to be dealt with first. I fear that automation will further bury these essential issues. Intractable problems are usually solved by being re-stated; their 'facts' are found to be irrelevant. Vast vested interests resist such re-statements; and I fear that automation will make these vaster still. Most of all, I fear the possibilities of automatized decision making, because I believe that the criteria which determine important decisions are only evolved by the process of decision itself and that this process, so tedious and necessarily only half-conscious, will be further jeopardized by the appearance of the new technique and the new mystique, with its panache of certainty. In so far as men necessarily become slaves to their techniques, this is the area in which slavery is most to be feared.

But why should men become the slaves of their own techniques? This is one of those questions which can only be answered by being re-stated. 'Slave or master' is not the choice between man and machine, any more than it is between man and man. These are extremes in a gamut of relations which are always mutual. The slave owner is moulded by his mastery, no less than the slave by his slavery; and so it is for all the relations between these extremes. We recognize this between man and man; we should recognize it also between man and machine, man and technique, man and institution. How powerfully were nineteenth century ideas of human relation moulded by mechanical concepts of energy and causation! Even human authority was conceived as akin to mechanical pushes and pulls. A world dominated by techniques of communication, accustomed to distinguish the flow of information from the flow of energy will be different from the world today in its thinking about all relationships. It will not necessarily be more human; but we can hope that it may.

The peopling of the world with self-regulating machines may teach us respect for self-regulation, which would be no small advance; it would at least set us an example better than the bulldozer. The limits of automation, when they appear, may remind us that there are human excellencies beyond problem solving. So there is promise as well as threat in the impact of automation on our conceptual world.

And this may be affected by my fourth impact area, the growth and structuring of that section of human life called leisure.

Industrialization produced a culture in which status as well as income came to depend very much on employment. Indeed, it was a matter of pride that industrialization dethroned status and replaced it by contract. The free man might become anything. By the same token, until he had become something, he was nothing. This trend, never of course complete, seems to have been reversed. We are busy re-building the status of the citizen as such. I doubt if the dominance of contract was ever accepted, except as an outrage, by any except the minority for whom work was not only a livelihood but a career. (Perhaps we are the poorer for the unavoidable fact that for nearly all successful sociologists work is a career.)

Now as the world of leisure develops from a mere interlude in work into an area large enough to need and generate its own significance – and of course it is already doing so – what shape will it take, what values will it evolve? It will be an unfamiliar social pattern. In the past the leisured class has been drawn from the rich; in the brave new world which is coming, only the rich, it seems, will be busy – or at least busy of necessity.

This leisured world has already some interesting characteristics. Its inhabitants 'do it themselves', partly for fun and partly because no one they can afford to pay will do it for them. No doubt they sometimes do it together and do it for each other. Will this expanding world of leisure generate a culture complementary to that imposed by the automata, who will increasingly populate the world of work? Such complementary cultures, even protest cultures, are not unknown today. Will it perhaps in time become more dominant than the world of work, become the cultural world in which all live, even though some 'go to work' from it? I think this unlikely and that automation makes it less likely.

The two conditions, leisure and unemployment, are radically different. Take leisure first. Both men and women can look forward to an increase in their hours of leisure, without prejudice to the interest and status and income which they derive from work. This is a welcome opportunity but the societies in which it arises are I think ill-formed, both physically and culturally, to encourage its use. They were formed by work and for work, by profit and for profit. A leisured urban society, for example, should live in cities in which the delights of leisure can be enjoyed, not in cities from which the citizens escape whenever leisure and traffic density allow. A leisured culture worth having would increase the demand for all those amenities which private industry does not supply. Urban planning is already a major unsolved problem in which the needs of men in movement increasingly defeat the needs of men at rest. Can we still further shift the balance of the mixed economy without turning it upside down? Values appropriate to such a leisured sector could not be developed without revolutionizing also the values of the world of work.

The other condition, endemic unemployment contains a far more blatant and familiar challenge. If, as I think is likely, automation, added to our current state, destroys the balance between jobs and production, not slightly and briefly by permanently and increasingly, one of two things, as it seems to me, must happen. Either we must find a way to assimilate unemployed people into the society of the employed on a basis of real equality; or we must find a way to distribute goods and services freely according to need; or both. Our societies may be adaptable enough to achieve such a radical solution but if so, they will themselves be transformed by the achievement.

Consider what would happen. Mounting long-term unemployment in our society would be a social and economic scandal far more disruptive now, rate for rate, than it was in the 30's. It would be a social scandal because we know and are sensitive to its social costs. It would be an economic scandal even more offensive now than thirty years ago, that men and women should be turned off as marginally uneconomic by a calculation which took no account of the public resources which they would claim. Governments would be moved to ever more novel measures to find these people the status of employment, however subsidized, rather than subsidize them direct. These measures would further erode the philosophy of the market; and they would not be enough. So governments would be equally impelled to try to assimilate the unemployed to the status of the leisured. This also would erode the philosophy of the market, but it could not, I think, succeed within the framework of that philosophy, however eroded; so these measures also would not be enough. There would emerge a 'displaced' eliminated class, which knew it was not wanted and felt that it did not belong. Such a class emerges very quickly, as we know to our cost; a few years is enough.

This class would have techniques of protest, as their fellow citizens would have areas of vulnerability, which were not there thirty years ago. As voters, as demonstrators, as pressure groups, let alone as revolutionaries, a minority need not be large to be effective if it has a sensitive spot to assail.

The threatening prospect disclosed by these speculations is a society sharply divided into three classes – an over-busy minority of technologists, possessing indispensable skills; an under-occupied majority, kept happy by commercially structured leisure; and a residue of uncertain size who live by preying on the other two, either as a less unsatisfying way of life or as a form of protest.

There is, of course, another way of distributing leisure and wealth. It is to maintain normal hours of work not far below their present level; to absorb the excess of work potential by lowering the age of compulsory retirement to fifty or even lower and providing for all on retirement pensions at least equal to their full earnings at retirement; and to look to this affluent band of not-so-elderly elders to do all the work not regarded by the system as economic; to help govern states and cities, run many of the public services; organize voluntary and leisure enterprises, patronize the arts, develop culture and the arts of living; in fact, to do everything which the leisured, independent class used to do in class-structured societies. In this two-phased but not two-class society, everyone would pass at middle age into a higher grade of social dignity and responsibility. There would at least be a chance that this post-work world might become the dominant, the more important and the more interesting half of social and individual life, served by an economic sector which had shrunk to a place appropriate to it in a post-scarcity age.

If the idea seems neither realistic nor attractive to you, it is worth wondering why. It does at least recognize that in a world of non-scarcity there will be things to do more difficult, more responsible and more important, than earning a living; things which the leisured have always done and which, until recently, they thought only the leisured could do; things which are today neglected. (Perhaps this is what makes it repellent.) I do not prophesy that this will happen; indeed, I think it most unlikely. But I have no doubt that whatever does happen will be at least as radical and probably far less attractive.

The position of Western societies in their own eyes and in the eyes of the world, depends on whether they can really master those deficiencies which, as I stated earlier, they have been patching for decades. Of course North America leads the world in productive techniques and the world will come to her to learn them. But can our Western societies distribute what is needed where it is needed without wrecking their productive or their social system? Can they control, direct and when necessary curb their own growth as their own needs require? Can they combine the liberties of their private sector with a social purpose sufficient to sustain them through crisis of radical change? These are the questions which matter and which will vividly be seen to matter, when automation, added to our present state of development, had made productivity itself a problem.

Automation poses these questions not only to Western societies but to all developed and developing societies, not least to the Soviet Union. Our histories and theirs will give our several answers and by our answers we shall be judged. In the course of those histories our cultural state and our institutional state will change; and so will theirs. For major adaptation takes place not only or chiefly in the world of know-how, in finding new means to old ends, in the fascinating monkey-world of techniques. It takes place also and far more radically in the world of ideas and values, which is the creation and the dwelling place of free men and in the institutional world through which alone those values are realized. Automation will be the occasion for radical adaptation not only in techniques but in our concepts, our values and our institutions.

What these will be, we can neither clearly discern nor perhaps even in theory predict; for the result depends on our own and our children's choices. I have suggested some conceptional impacts which seem to me a threat, others which perhaps hold a promise. If we can withstand the threats and realize the promises, we may yet use this vast innovation to make a world more human, not less human than today's, by which I mean a world in which more of us are more free and more ready to prize and exercise the most characteristic activities of being human; skill, appreciation, sympathy, delight and wonder.

REFERENCES

[1] Jaques, E., *The Measurement of Responsibility*. (1956) London: Tavistock Publications.
[2] Wiener, N., *The Human Use of Human Beings*. (1950) Boston: Houghton Mifflin Co., p. 56.

CHAPTER TEN

Industry, Human Relations and Mental Health*

I THINK the best way to explore the very general subject which has been given to me is to try to answer three questions. First, what do we mean by 'human relations in industry'? Secondly, in what ways do these relations differ from human relations in other social contexts – for instance, in the family or the national society? Thirdly, to what extent is it useful to appraise these relations by criteria of mental health, rather than by the more usual criteria of individual prosperity or industrial efficiency or economic growth? None of the answers is obvious or uncontroversial.

An observer from another planet, endowed with power to see all our economic activities displayed before him in space and time, would get an impression of immensely complex but not random activity. He would notice countless centres to which people flocked daily and through which flowed, in varying volumes, streams of material, money, and information. He would, for example, be fascinated to watch Antarctic whale-oil and tropical ground-nuts converging and mingling to become margarine in European larders. When he had taken in the whole picture, he would realize that the greater part of the whole product was consumed, as food or fuel, in providing the energy needed to keep the process going, while the rest replaced and on balance enlarged the total stock of human artifacts on the planet. He would sense a subtle net of co-ordination which regulated these flows but he would have no means of guessing what it was. If he asked

*An address given at the seventeenth annual meeting of the World Federation for Mental Health, in 1964.

us, the most complete answer we could give in two words would be 'human relations'; for we could not explain the workings of the commodity markets or the stock market, let alone the self-maintaining activity of an individual undertaking, without reference to a vast underlying system of mutual human expectations, embodied in complementary human roles.

If this planetary visitor focused his attention on a single factory, he would see the same process in miniature. He would notice material of many kinds flowing from many sources towards the centre, where part, the fuel, for example, would be consumed; part would be absorbed into the productive equipment; and part would pass through the fabricating process and flow out again as finished products or as scrap.

He would notice that this stream of materials was made up of constituents flowing at different rates. Materials might be processed in a few weeks, machines would last for a few years, buildings for some decades; but ultimately even the channels through which the material flows would be revealed as themselves transient, processes rather than structures, destined in time to be replaced by others. The entire assembly would appear in its true light as a process not unlike a candle flame but more complex; for the 'steady state' representing the balance between inflow and outflow may wax and wane without imbalance and is composed of constituents flowing at different rates.

Parallel with this flow but opposite in direction, would be observed the flow of money, inwards from consumers and outwards to suppliers, employees, and providers of capital; and this flow also would fluctuate in volume. Even the human beings whose activities keep all these tides flowing would be seen to obey the same law. Any individual watched for long would disappear from his accustomed place, to re-appear elsewhere or not at all; and his place would be taken by another. Viewed as an organization of people, the enterprise would appear as a stream of men and women, flowing into, through, and out of the undertaking through invisible but enduring channels.

At this point the planetary visitor might well turn to us, perhaps with embarrassing expressions of admiration and respect and ask –

'How does it work? What ensures that these flows shall be maintained at their appropriate relative rates, overall and in detail, notwithstanding these frequent changes of personnel?' Our first answer might be to produce the organization chart. These people, we might say, are organized in a hierarchy of sub-systems. Each department is responsible for maintaining some aspect of this dynamic balance; for processing, for marketing, for recruitment and promotion of staff, for financial control, and so on. Within each department, each place, from the director to the cleaner, has its allotted role, consisting of duties and discretions which are expected of the holder and rights which he is entitled to expect from the holders of other roles. This pattern of complementary roles distributes responsibility for action, establishes channels of communication, and makes it possible for large numbers of people to combine in complicated and enduring operations, even though few of them have even a summary notion of what is being done.

We should have explained only a fraction of this extraordinary business. The visitor has seen the factory from the viewpoint of the manager but he has not seen what the manager sees; still less has he felt what the manager feels. For the manager is not only the centre of the regulative system which governs the internal and external relations of the undertaking. He is also an individual agent, to whom the undertaking is the means of support for himself and his family; one source, perhaps the greatest, of his status and success, in the eyes of himself and others; the principal outlet for his energies; his principal social milieu; and the focus of his professional interests as an engineer and a manager. This is equally true of every individual agent in the system. Each man, be he on the assembly belt, in the drawing office, behind the controls of a crane, or in the manager's chair, is a separate, unique world, maintaining and depending on an unique set of relations with his milieu, including the social milieu provided by his fellows, and finds in it and in them his stresses and his supports. Only some of these relations are implicit in his role and even these have for him a significance different from their meaning for the undertaking. The social unit which the sociologist observes is never visible to any of the agents who compose it, except perhaps by an intellectual effort which none can maintain for long; nor is their vision accessible to him, except by an intuitive sharing of experience which is open to him not because he is a sociologist, still less because he is a scientist, but simply because he is human.

Let us simplify this inquiry by concentrating on three main aspects of the industrial agent's role. He has relations with his working group, including his immediate superior and his subordinates, if he has any. He has relationships with his employer, as the source of his income and the controller of his future employment, his promotion, and the conditions of his work. He also has relations with his trade union or professional or occupational group. This triple subdivision holds good for nearly all in industry, whatever their role, though those whose roles are primarily regulative are associated in the working group in a manner different from that of the operatives.

In all these relations I will distinguish personal relations, such as exist between a man and those of whom he is conscious as individuals, from other human relations such as those which he has with more remote persons and organizations, relations which, though human, are not personal. Remote directors may be wholly impersonal to an employee whose livelihood their decisions affect but the employee knows well enough that they are human, open to the pressures and persuasions which distinguish human interaction. So he may refuse to accept some fruits of human decision that he would accept without question if they were the result of natural forces. We can bear blind fate better than a blind boss. On the other hand, human relations may be highly supportive, even when they are non-personal. It is the merit of a role structure that it can support human expectations across the gulf which would otherwise be created by changing personalities.

So I would answer my first question as follows. By human relations in industry I mean all those relations between people which are implicit in industrial roles, whether between worker and worker, worker and supervisor, worker and employer, or any others related hierarchically or laterally in the organization; and I include both inter-personal relations and those larger-scale relations which are impersonal but still human. An extreme example of these is reached in negotiations between an organized industry on the one hand and a national organization of workers on the other, negotiations which may be intensely personal between the negotiators but which involve and are limited by their relations with perhaps millions of others, to whom the negotiators on both sides are an impersonal but highly human 'they'.

Human relations in industry are sharply distinguishable from human relations in any other social system in our Western culture, for reasons that are partly inherent and partly an unhappy legacy of history.

Industry involves more extensive division of labour, more deliberate co-ordination of policy, and more rapid and radical changes in the volume and direction of effort than any other human activity of our time, except war. It must therefore require to an exceptional degree among its participants acceptance of role, exchange of information, and mutual trust, especially perhaps the last. For in industry, even more than in politics, the normal feedback cycle, whereby experience and anticipation alert us to the need for change, is fragmented. Trends visible from the board-room may need action on the factory floor – and consequently disruption of familiar behaviour patterns and perhaps serious disturbance to individuals – years before the need for them becomes apparent to those who must give effect to them and to those who will suffer by them. Conversely, troubles on the factory floor may be obvious and clamant to those on the spot years before they can be dealt with by an echelon high enough to make the changes that they demand. In industry, then, above nearly all other social systems, people have to vary their action, often to their own inconvenience or even detriment, in reliance on the judgment of others; others often above them but sometimes below them in the hierarchy. Yet in this complex but flexible organization all the roles are deliberately designed; they are allotted and changed by the holders of roles above them in the hierarchy; and they are occupied transiently by successive holders, each associated formally only by a contract of employment. The right of the employer to design and change the size and shape of his role structure and to choose and change successive role-holders is as jealously guarded as the right of the employee to choose and change his job.

To combine flexibility and co-ordination on such a scale, the most obvious way is to make industrial roles easy to learn and easy to inspect and to reduce in each of them the content of discretion and the amount of information and mutual trust that the holder needs to do his job.

In earlier days these goals were pursued by industry to a degree which proved self-defeating. Today industry is busy reversing these earlier mistakes; seeking to build into its workers' roles enough discretion, enough use of information, and enough co-operation to provide an acceptable occupation for a human being. Yet even if industry were free from the traditions of the past, it would still be bound by these inherent limitations. It is useless to design an industrial role requiring of its holder skills, habits, or attitudes that cannot be found ready made or quickly learned by those who will successively fill it.

One way in which roles can be simplified and made less dependent on the ability of their transient holders is to stress the authoritarian nature of the hierarchy and to rely increasingly on direction from above. Here again industry in the past carried the principle to a self-defeating point and is now busy correcting the mistake; yet here again authority can be dispensed with only to a limited extent. It is inescapable in a type of organization such as I have described that relations up and down the hierarchy should play a larger part than in social systems less concerned to achieve co-ordinated yet flexible action on a large scale.

These, then, I suggest, are the inherent peculiarities of industrial organizations and hence of the human relations of which they are composed. Roles are less socially sanctioned than those of most other social systems; they are allotted by contract, rather than by custom; and they contain a more than usually large proportion of relations involving subordination or superordination to the holders of other roles in a hierarchy. Even newly developing countries, which are happily at liberty to evolve a system of industrial roles free from the historic legacy under which Western societies labour, will be forced, I think, to accept these facts and the limitations they involve.

In Western countries, these difficulties are magnified by the legacy of a past which implicitly denied much of what we now believe to be true and important in the field of human relations. This may apply especially to my own country, which, being early in the field, absorbed into its industrial system an especially large element of nineteenth-century concepts and values; but I understand that these handicaps are not unknown elsewhere. I will distinguish three. First, proud of an age which was replacing status by contract, our ancestors did not realize that aggregates of human beings, assembled like aggregates of machinery or of capital through 'the market', would none the less insist on becoming, for good or ill, social systems; must indeed become social systems if they were to function adequately; and that, though contract might be a welcome passport to status, it could never be a substitute. Secondly, their minds were dominated by mechanical analogies of a kind which seem infinitely crude even to the technology of today; so they conceived of human organizations as operated by 'pushes and pulls' and devised a 'kick and carrot' psychology of corresponding crudity. Thirdly, by equating labour with other commodities and creating a 'free market' through which to distribute it, they built into the vertical relations in the business hierarchy a relationship inherently incompatible with that which the working of the system would require.

Since then the business world has changed past recognition. Its still nominally 'private' institutions have become the focus of complex public responsibilities; they are expected and even expect themselves to sustain external relationships, as employers, suppliers of services, earners of foreign exchange, land users, and so on, in accordance with norms of behaviour undreamed of a few decades ago. They are even more concerned to humanize their internal relations, partly in response to public expectation but partly also in response to the need to become social systems sufficiently effective and responsive to survive. Even their machines are increasingly controlled by signals, rather than by pushes and pulls, that is to say by the passing of information, rather than by the transmission of energy; and this is helping to make acceptable more true and sophisticated ideas about the control and self-control of men.

But the inertia of the past, our safeguard in adversity, is a drag on the wheel when we would reverse our mistakes. The ghosts of the past walk so freely through our minds that we can hardly tell them from our friends. One example must suffice. A free market meant to our grandfathers a market containing so many buyers and so many sellers that no one of them could affect it. It provided an independent criterion of value in the market price only because this expressed the result of numberless individual choices. In this sense the free market has virtually ceased to exist in any field and especially in the so-called labour market. Yet in national wage negotiations in my country and in others too a single buyer and a single seller, partners in what is in fact an indissoluble partnership, still sit down to what is described as 'collective bargaining'; and if they fail to agree, an arbitrator, applying no known law yet going through the forms of judicial inquiry, produces an award, after hearing arguments in which the medieval idea of 'the just price' figures far more prominently than the supposedly governing idea of the market price. In taking part in such 'negotiations' I have sometimes felt as if I were assisting at some late form of medieval tourney, in which, under the ritual forms of combat, some new procedure was quietly taking shape.

Let me summarize my answer to my second question. Human relations in industry are not different in kind from human relations in any other social context but they are different in degree; partly because industrial activity necessarily requires an organization more hierarchic and more authoritarian than most other social activities and thus depends to an unusual extent on acceptance of role, ability to handle information, and, especially, on mutual trust; and partly because the legacy of history makes these conditions especially hard to create.

It remains for me to answer my third question. What are the significant aspects of this complex of human relations that we call industry, when we regard it not as a means of providing goods or distributing incomes but from the viewpoint of mental health?

We are not here as industrialists asking what has mental health to do with industry. We are asking what has industry to do with mental health. I need therefore spend no time describing industry's need for men and women free from mental illness and possessing the skills and the stability of personality which are commonly identified with mental health. Nor need I recount the shocking estimates of man-hours lost through mental illness, let alone the less measurable, but probably greater, losses which come from attitudes that can be called psychopathological.

Nor have I been asked to explore the effect on mental health of the industrialization which is transforming our world at an accelerating rate, though these are for mental health far the most significant changes of our time. They produce far denser and more rapidly growing populations, far more rapid changes in the physical and hence in the cultural milieu than have ever before been known or dreamed of; and, in doing so, they cramp our living space, frustrate our expectations, depreciate our skills, make nonsense of our experience as a basis for prediction, condemn our institutions to perpetual obsolescence, if not ineptitude, and destroy the cultural assurances by which we live. This accelerating spin into chaos will not be mitigated by any change, however welcome, in relations *within* industry; and it could be controlled, if at all, only by changes in the organization and culture of our Western societies which could be barely compassed in the time available to us, even if the only powers that could achieve them were not committed to resist them.

All this constitutes, in my view, a threat to mental health so huge as to dwarf any other; but, happily perhaps, it is not within my subject. I am concerned not with the impact of industrialization, as now organized and controlled, on Western society, but with the effect on individual mental health of participating in the human relations which that organization now involves. Even this is a vast subject. I will consider briefly the three areas of relationship that I distinguished earlier. Consider first relations within the working group. The psychological hazards commonly recognized here are too much dictation from outside and from above and hence too little opportunity for self-direction; too much fragmentation of work function and hence too little satisfaction in creative achievement, whether individual or collective; and too little support and enjoyment through human co-operation. Never, it might be said, did so many men co-operate so closely to produce such marvellous artifacts; and never did they get less satisfaction either from the experience of co-operation or from the experience of creation.

This, though far from wholly true, has more truth than it need have or should have in our Western societies today. It is in part due to the attempt to make industrial roles 'foolproof', easily assimilable by a succession of holders with no high degree of skill or motivation. As I have already pointed out, the obvious way to do this is to minimize the dependence of each role on experience, information, and mutual trust, to set the tempo through the machine and to supply the co-ordination from above. This trend has produced types of organization that industry already recognizes as inefficient. Fascinating studies in the British coal industry, for example.[1] have shown the danger of associating men in technical interdependence which does not permit the growth of a corresponding sense of social interdependence; as when coal-getting is organized in a twenty-four-hour cycle of three shifts which never meet.

This danger may perhaps be less with more advanced technology. Changes in the organization of coal-getting, made possible, and indeed necessary, by the full mechanisation of the process, not only permit but require more socially integrated teams, responsible for less fragmented work. There is still a large field in which even our present knowledge of the psychological needs of men at work can point the way both to greater efficiency and to conditions more favourable to mental health. The conditions of mental health, however, cannot be left solely to the enlightened pursuit of efficiency, any more than can the conditions of physical health. I hope that the pursuit of them for their own sake will not be based on too limited a view of the variety and adaptability of men. There is room for team jobs and solitary jobs, regular jobs and jobs irregular in their hours and their demands, exacting jobs and jobs of the simplest routine.

I turn to the second field, the relations of men in industry with their employer. This field is shadowed by the insecurity of industrial work, derived from the uncertainty of employment and sharpened by the fact that continued employment depends on the unfettered discretion of some other role-holder. We should not underestimate this insecurity. The number of unemployed is no clear index of the fear of unemployment; nor is this fear limited to some lower echelons of the pyramid especially in the older age groups, where adequate provision for retirement is still exceptional, if 'adequacy' is taken to mean what may secure a reasonable man from anxiety. I know of no evidence to show that uncertainty is of itself inimical to mental health; wartime experience suggests that the reverse may sometimes be true. Yet memories of the 30's should leave us in no doubt of the dangers that result (both to individuals and to society) when individuals are displaced from society through unemployment which no personal initiative of theirs can avert. The unemployed of those days foreshadowed the problem of the displaced person, a problem made more challenging by the fact that they were displaced within their own community. We have not yet shown, nor have we reason to hope, that we can banish unemployment in the automated future or that we can distribute it as leisure in any form compatible with our present ideas of status and success. Indeed, there is every reason to think that industry as now organized will progressively cease to be an acceptable producer or distributor of *jobs*, as distinct from goods. The problem of the displaced person is the greatest growing problem of our industrialized societies; and it is a problem of mental health. In this alienated and atomized world we are all more or less displaced persons.

It is the employer, whether public or private, who distributes, enhances, or withdraws this privilege of working and with it the most essential status our society has to offer; and he does so in the course of regulating a system primarily governed by other and unrelated requirements. The existence of this power, whether used or not, is bound to charge with stress the whole relationship between those who can exercise it and those who are subject to it, and this stress is bound to increase as the implicit threat becomes, for whatever reason, more serious. It is further amplified by all the resonances with which it has been charged by a century of industrial strife. The political and legal rights to which we are born, precious as they are, are psychologically less protective and supportive than are the social rights, inherent in many cultures, including our own at an earlier date, which are our birthright no more.

I turn to the third area, the field of relations subsisting between a man and his occupational or professional group. These have always had, and have today, strong supportive significance for their members; it is one of their major objectives. The organizations which subserve them have always served, among other things, to protect the group against attack or attrition from without and to support its status against other competing groups. In our modern industrial world this function has grown in relative importance. Many trade unions exist for no other purpose and are structurally inept for any other purpose.

For the historical reasons I have mentioned this field includes large areas of institutionalized combat. These include relations not only between organized employers and organized employees but also between rival organizations of the employed. These bellicose attitudes are too crude for the needs of societies in such peril as I have described. Industrialists, politicians, ordinary citizens, even some trade unionists view them with justified alarm. They are open to criticism in many ways. Whether they are bad for mental health is, I think, less clear. A fight is a refreshingly simple and supportive situation; in few other circumstances do we have so many comrades and so few doubts. If our industrial societies relapse into patterns of increasingly unqualified conflict, as their problems become ever less amenable to more integrative solutions, it will be a symptom of large-scale disaster; but from an individual viewpoint it may none the less be the least bad psychological defence available. Let us not make mental health the scapegoat, if we fail to grapple with the problems we have generated.

And yet – this is a field in which mental health is equally relevant; for whether we are speaking of mental health or of general public health – of which, I hold, mental health is an inseparable part – we should not describe conditions of health only in terms of freedom from hazard.

Health, physical or mental, is a function of three variables – the hazards of the milieu, the support of the milieu, and the immunity (or resistance) of the individual. The relation between the three can be clearly seen in the attack on infectious disease, that prototype of public health activity. Its earliest efforts were towards the reduction of hazard – clean water, efficient drainage, antisepsis – but it has won its successes at least as much by building up immunity, both specifically, by increasing resistance to particular diseases, and generally, by improved diet and living conditions. It started from two biologically given facts, the variable vulnerability of the human constitution to infective organisms and the increase of these organisms in the conditions of urban living; and its task has been to find a *cultural* solution which would so match man and his milieu as to hold infectious illnesses at an acceptable level.

This task is wider than the commonly accepted field of public health. Today, in our search for what in my country is called social security, sickness of all kinds is only one of 'five giant evils', identified as major enemies of human well-being. Again the solution sought is a cultural one, in which the age-old threats of sickness, ignorance, unemployment, squalor, and want may be held at an acceptable level, partly by reducing their incidence and partly by increasing the personal and social resources of those who must cope with them. The second of these approaches is proving just as essential and much more elusive than the first.

Mental health is an inseparable constituent of public health; and industry is an inseparable part of our culture. We know relatively little in this field about the nature of the three variables, hazard, protection, and immunity; and even less about how to control them. They are all the more essential as landmarks, marking out three fields of inquiry, none of which can be ignored or resolved into the others, though none can usefully be studied in isolation.

Industry will always present some hazard to health, including mental health, as will all the activities of life. It is the responsibility of our culture, including the industrial sub-culture that forms part of it, not only to minimize these hazards and to increase the supports that can avert or mitigate the breakdowns of the vulnerable, but also to foster in the individual the power to preserve that internal stability which, as Claude Bernard observed long ago, is the condition of free and independent life. When Bernard spoke of '*la stabilité du milieu intérieur*' he was not thinking of psychological maturity; yet if we were to adopt his famous phrase as a partial definition of mental health, we should make clear to every manager what mental health has to do with that singular net of human relations which we call industry.

REFERENCE

[1] Trist, E. L., Higgin, G. W., Murray, H. and Pollock, A. B., *Organizational Choice; Capabilities of Groups at the Coal Face under Changing Technologies.* (1963) London: Tavistock Publications.

CHAPTER ELEVEN

Adaptation as a Management Concept*

THE RESPONSIBILITIES of management are largely determined by what people come to expect of it; and today two large bodies of expectation are growing apace. As producers, we expect far more of industry than we did. We expect it to provide for us not only a livelihood but a satisfying way of life; a career, if we are ambitious; all the training and education we need for our chosen path (but of course no compulsion as to what we choose); security in all its forms, combined with abundant opportunity; ever more pay for less effort; and a pension at the end. Each of these objectives is in itself legitimate, and each is attainable in some measure and at some cost, but as a bundle of aspirations it far exceeds anything which any previous age has dreamed of demanding from industry and hence it represents a notable addition to the responsibilities of management.

Another equally formidable body of expectations has grown up, focused upon our status as consumers. We expect industry to supply us every day, year by year, with an increasing flow of necessities and luxuries at prices so related to our earnings that by and large we can continually enjoy more of them. And since we are at last awake to the fact that we get even our necessities only by exchange, our expectations of management include the expectation that it will retain its competitive position in the world sufficiently to make this ever-increasing increment possible. Thus we have added to management an explicit responsibility to society as consumer for its relative and absolute efficiency in terms of response to demand and value for money.

How far are these two bodies of expectation, and hence of responsibility, consistent with each other? We all know that management in

*First published in January 1958.

the last century overlooked the social character of industry so gravely as to prejudice its own efficiency; and there was a happy era when changes in management concepts which were justified on grounds of social welfare, social justice, even plain humanity, proved again and again to be equally justified in terms of industrial efficiency. Men often produced more, not less, when their hours were shortened – from twelve to ten, from ten to eight. Sometimes they produced more in five days than in six. To realize the one set of expectations proved a royal road to realizing the other.

There is no reason to suppose that this will always be true. On the contrary, there are a hundred ways in which our legitimate expectations as producers conflict with our equally legitimate expectations as consumers. Economically it is desirable that expensive plant should be worked continuously; but socially it is desirable that people should work, rest and play at the same times and not in shifts.

Socially, the aspiration for a month's holiday is as legitimate in a miner as in a company director; but economically the cost in coal of a week's holiday for miners is such that after nationalization the miners' union deferred for some years their claim to raise their one week's holiday to two. Instances could be multiplied indefinitely. There is, no doubt, much still to do which will serve equally to further the aspirations of producers and of consumers, and some of it may still be hidden from us by the same fear and ignorance which have so often been proved wrong before. But we deceive ourselves if we ignore the fact that the two paths are diverging now and are likely to diverge still more with every new advance.

Management is confronted with the task of reconciling expectations which grow ever greater and less consistent. Contrast this with the responsibility of management as it was commonly conceived only a few decades ago. Management was expected to hire men, like other resources, as cheaply and to sell its product as profitably as might be. The magic of the market was relied on to transmute these base metals into the gold of well-being, narrowly conceived but passionately believed in, for consumers and producers alike; and the market was the ultimate Court of Appeal. We have moved a long way since then.

We have not only lost some of our faith in the magic of the market; the free market itself, in its original sense, is becoming a thing of the past. Neither the labour market nor the commodity market is, over important areas, a free market in the old sense. Correspondingly, we are developing a sense of responsibility, real though vague, to do for the employee and the consumer what the market was once supposed to do.

The present situation is transitional and full of contradictions. Wage negotiations still take the form of a market bargain, even though more often than not there is only one buyer and one seller. Over whole industries, in default of agreement, the issue is submitted to an arbitrator, legally trained and observing the formalities of a law court but applying no known law; and in the arguments before him the medieval concept of a 'just' price and the nineteenth-century concept of a market price jostle each other with no apparent sense of inconsistency.

The responsibility of management to the public as consumers is still more transitional. Many, perhaps most, products are still sold to realize the highest profit obtainable; but the safeguard of a free market diminishes as sellers grow larger and fewer. Alternative safeguards, such as nationalization and the Monopolies and Restrictive Practices Commission, come slowly to birth, and are applicable only to specific parts of the immense field. Meantime, the climate of management opinion undergoes changes which are subtle, gradual and hard to chart. I find it impossible to guess what that climate will be even ten years hence, when the rival and inconsistent claims of these two growing bodies of expectation have been crystallized by constant head-on collision in the public consciousness, in the board-room, across the table of negotiation, and in the numberless contexts which associate organized management, organized labour and government, with each other and with public opinion, increasingly organized in defence of the consumer.

Yet the situation is in no way new; it is a commonplace of life. Every organization, like every organism, has to reconcile two separate but related sets of problems. It has to regulate the inner forces by which it hangs together, and it has to regulate the relation between itself and its environment. Since an organization, like an organism, is an 'open' system, surviving only through constant interchange with its environment, its inner and outer relations are interdependent; failure of either will destroy the other. Yet the problems of inner and outer coherence present themselves as separate problems.

An animal must learn to find the food it can digest or learn to digest the food it can find, or both; and it survives only so long as its capacity for adaptation in both these directions combined makes possible a viable compromise between its needs and its opportunities. The same is true of men and organizations of men at all levels. The problem of management in reconciling these rival and growing bodies of expectation from men as producers and from the same men as consumers, is only another example of the challenge to adapt which is inherent in life.

It is not on that account necessarily soluble. Both organisms and organizations frequently perish because they cannot respond adequately to the challenges which come their way. When they thus fail, their place is taken by other organisms or organizations better fitted to deal with the new situation.

Now there has been of late a great extension in the knowledge and the conceptual apparatus available to us for picturing and even predicting the response of such systems to their conflicting inner and outer demands. This comes partly from biological sources, partly from the study of social and economic systems, partly from the body of theory which has been developed in relation to the design of electronic devices for computation and control. These ways of thinking are beginning to affect our lay concept of how organizations work and of the limited but important part which we can play in influencing their behaviour – and hence our ideas of the responsibilities of management. I shall use a few ideas from these sources which seem to me to be helpful in picturing to ourselves the nature of the conflict to which I have pointed, the conditions under which it can be resolved and the part which management might play in the process.

I propose to try to focus what adaptation means when applied to business management, because a main task of management is to see that the organization it manages is 'adaptive'; and if our concept of adaptation is changing there are likely to be parallel changes in our concepts of management.

If the world will not give me what I want, I can react in any or all of four different ways. I can try to alter my wants; I can try to alter the world; I can hunt for new ways of pursuing my wants; I can bang my head on the floor and scream. Any of the first three rank as adaptive behaviour and nearly every situation calls for a combination of the three. Only the fourth is non-adaptive; among individuals it is called neurotic. Corporations have no heads to bang on floors, but non-adaptive, 'neurotic' behaviour is just as possible and just as common in collective as in individual behaviour, and it appears in management at all levels.

Consider the first three. An industrial concern which is being priced out of existence can try to make a price agreement with its competitors; that is, to alter the world, the environment outside itself. Or it can abandon the attempt to make a living in its existing line of business and try another; that is, to alter its own 'wants'. Or it can buy new equipment and take a dose of work study and generally try to be more efficient; in other words it can pursue its old goals in a new way. All three ways involve alterations to itself.

Now let me turn to the second and third of my forms of adaptiveness. We can adapt either by changing our wants or by finding new ways to satisfy the old wants. We have to be clear what is the difference between these two, because the first sets us a much harder task of adaptation than the second. You may say that this is the difference between means and ends. But that difference is notoriously hard to understand, even in speaking of an individual; and it is even harder when we are thinking about business undertakings, because a new policy which for part of the undertaking seems only a change of means may seem a change of ends to some other part. Thus to make an old product by new methods may mean a revolution in the production shop, while to make a new product by the old methods may scarcely raise a ripple there; but the effect on the sales force is likely to be the other way round.

The distinction between ends and means is, I think, unnecessarily confusing and I propose now to forget it. There is a better way of defining the difference between these two sorts of adaptation.

Take an illustration from biology. Analogies between organisms and organizations must not be carried too far but the one I shall use is, I think valid so far as I take it. We can define a creature by stating what it must and must not do and what it can and cannot do. Even its anatomy is something which it does: it builds and maintains itself just that way and no other; it cannot help it. Similarly, it has to exchange matter with its environment at its own metabolic rate; if it lets the rate of exchange fall too far below that rate, it dies of hunger or thirst or suffocation, according to the character of its failure. The higher animals have a host of such conditions which they have to maintain and their deviations from these have thresholds which they must not transgress on pain of death; and they spend most of their time pursuing the one and evading the other. I will call these positive governors 'norms' and the negative ones 'limits'. I shall suggest that organizations also are controlled by the norms they pursue and the limits they avoid.

Viewed from the purely financial angle, the economists assert that the norm which is sought is the rate of exchange with the environment which will yield the most profit; and though that would be strictly true only in a world peopled by economic men, it illustrates what I mean by a norm. At the other extreme we are all familiar with the limits beyond which a business cannot stray without suffering sudden, complete and irreversible change. Thus a business which is getting short of money has increasing difficulties with its credit and creditors; but up to a point these are matters of degree. If, however, things reach such a pass that the bank will not cash the weekly wages cheque. the trouble overflows suddenly into all the activities of the organization and brings it to a stop. All dynamic systems operate within similar limits, beyond which a new situation arises – the animal dies, the skater falls, the machine breaks, the business goes bankrupt.

I call these governors norms and limits, rather than positive or negative goals or ends, because a goal or end is usually something which can be attained once for all, whereas these norms and limits cannot be attained or escaped once for all. They are more like states of balance and imbalance. We have a troublesome habit of mind which makes us think of attainable ends as something final, whereas, so long as we are alive, no attainable end can be final, since it gives no guidance as to where we go when we have attained it. The only inexhaustible guides in a continuous, dynamic process are not goals but courses. Paradoxical though it may seem, in any continuing activity courses are more fundamental than goals. The man who steers by some sea-mark, however distant, will pass it some time and need another mark; but the man who steers by the North Star does not expect to reach and pass it and would hate to do so, for he would be lost if he did.

In the same way, a business is governed fundamentally not by the desire to attain specific goals and avoid specific threats, but by the need to maintain or avoid particular relationships. The salesman's efforts to make a series of particular sales is only the expression of his need to maintain or attain a particular volume of sales per unit of time; that is, to maintain or attain a given rate of interchange with the outisde world, just as the successive catching of particular rabbits by a fox is only a means to the maintenance of its metabolic balance. The same is true of all other business activities.

Animals and men have a limited repertory of things which they can do in pursuing their norms and avoiding their limits and limited skill in using them; and the same is true of organizations. I will borrow the biological word and call these 'responses', though it is not a very happy word even in biology. So the 'nature' of animals and men – and, I am suggesting, of organizations also – is defined by stating their norms and limits, that is, the states, courses, conditions, which they must hold or must avoid, and the responses and skills at their disposal in this endless task. And this is the distinction I am seeking between the two sorts of internal adjustment. To change our 'wants' is to alter our norms and limits. To find new ways to attain our wants is to add to our repertory of responses or our skill in using them.

An animals's norms and limits are for the most part built into it and are not chargeable in the space of a lifetime. Adaptation at this level occurs only genetically over many generations. The norms and limits which govern a business corporation are for the most part less rigid; most of them can change widely in the course of its existence. But their maximum rate of change is also governed by a time factor.

Take, for example, a company making automobiles. What is it trying to do? To make automobiles? To make money? Neither seems to me an adequate description of the norm which shapes its policy. If you ask the people in the development department what lines they are following in designing a new model, you will find that they are trying to combine a number of requirements as to performance, appearance, size and price; and these in turn are designed to catch at least so much of a particular market. This in turn is part of a long-term policy to maintain the company as an effective supplier of an adequate part of the automobile market.

Even this is not an ultimate norm. The company could make motors other than for automoblies: it could make machinery other than motors; it could in time change its activities out of all recognition. One of our great steel-makers began by making hobnails in a backyard; and one of their most successful phases was supplying corrugated iron sheet to a world market which now has almost passed away. Today it is steel sheet, tomorrow who knows what?

Clearly the time dimension is crucial to the concept of adaptation. In our example of the automobile factory, today's norms and limits are built into the tooling of the machines, the lay-out of the assembly lines. This organized activity is directed to producing a particular model in given numbers. Seen in a perspective of days or weeks, even months, there is no room to manoeuvre. But looking two to five years ahead the position is more fluid, while looking decades ahead almost anything can happen.

If you ask what *is* a particular business enterprise and if you look

indefinitely far ahead, you can say that it is an activity directed to maintaining a given relationship between a group of producers and the
general body of consumers, the essential of the relationship being that
the group shall produce what the consumers effectively want on such
terms as will secure the survival of the group. The members of the
group may change, and so may its assets, its tools, its place of work, its
product; but so long as this condition is maintained, it will go on and
will be regarded as a continuing entity.

At this point one cannot help asking whether this continuity is an
illusion. If everything changes, what endures? We attribute continuity
not only to things which remain unchanged but also to things which
change in the characteristic ways we know as growth, development
and, within limits, decay. I once attended a party given by a large and
famous corporation – call it A, B, and Co – to celebrate its twenty-first
birthday, and I paid a compliment to the secretary for the way his
office did its business. He said, 'Twenty-one years ago there were only
three people in this firm – Mr A, Mr B and me. Pretty well every job
in the firm was done by me at some time before it was hived offf.' Such
undertakings have a very strong sense of corporate existence, of continuity and mutual belonging, despite – or because of – their high rate
of change.

This suggests that the continuity of a business is the continuity – not
the changelessness – of the human relations which compose it. A business enterprise, like any other human activity, is a way of behaving,
a structure of mutual expectations, attached not to persons but rather
to roles. Its continuity lies in the fact that these expectations continue
to hold; when they change, the changes are understood, so that they
do not interrupt the mutual relations which they exist to further. In
the growth of A, B, and Co the one-time office-boy-factotum played
many roles and created many new ones, as new functions were distinguished and new people found to do them. These developments did not
disrupt the growing organization but on the contrary sharpened its
sense of corporate existence.

So when we look for the norms and limits which define a business
as a dynamic system we must seek them also among the laws which

govern growth and change in human relationships. Just as there are inescapable limits to the speed at which a new model can be tooled up, so there may be – and indeed there are – limits to the speed at which relationships between men can be changed without disruption. These are much more complex and we know less about them; but we should on that account take them more seriously. We seldom do so. We tend to start from the assumption that men 'ought' to be infinitely pliable, able and ready to change their ways of doing things and their relations with each other, once the need to do so has been presented to their reason – or even without this formality. We accept the logistic limitations of the tool-room but not the logistic limitations of the tool-maker. This attitude is without justification in view even of the little we know about how men behave.

The personalities of individuals are also systems, governed by norms and limits far more numerous and subtle than we know; and they are organized in work groups, each of which is also in greater or lesser degree a system, governed by its own norms and having its own stabilities to guard, its own limits to observe. An undertaking also, however small, is a hierarchy of overlapping systems, in which adaptation anywhere involves adaptation everywhere.

Adaptation for a business is twofold. It involves maintaining the external relationship of the undertaking with the consuming world within the limits set by economics and maintaining the internal relationships between the members and groups which form the enterprise, so that they will maintain the effectiveness and adaptability of the whole and provide for their own continuance.

To translate these generalities into the familiar facts of business management, I want now to consider the process by which these governors regulate the behaviour of men and societies and guide their adaptation.

The process by which norms and limits control us is fairly familiar. They provide a measure whereby we can tell where we ought to be – or, where the control is negative, where we ought not to be – for comparison with where we are. The deviation from the norm or the approach to the limit as the case may be gives the signal for corrective action. The classic example of such positive control is the control of a helmsman by the course on the compass card; and many of the statistical and financial returns which furnish the controls of business work the same way. Control by budget and forecast supplies at every level and at frequent intervals a measure of what 'ought to be' for comparison with what is. Without such guidance the operator is working in the dark; he has no means to measure his success or failure. Psychological inquiry has shown that a measure of success is as important internally as externally, if the individual is to be effective.

Consider more closely how this kind of control works. The helmsman reads from the compass from moment to moment the difference between his actual course and the course he has been set; the difference between the 'is' and the 'ought-to-be'; and by successive observations he can calculate the rate at which the one is approaching or deviating from the other. This widening or narrowing difference is the signal upon which he acts in moving the helm. His change of helm, along with all the other factors affecting the ship's course, is reflected soon afterwards by further changes on the compass card and these move him to further movements of the wheel. The process is the same when the helmsman's place is taken by an automatic pilot.

In the same way the information the manager receives about production, orders, sales, prices, costs or stocks is only useful if he can compare it with what it 'ought to be', that is, with what he would expect it to be, if things were going according to expectation: hence the importance which is attached to setting up standards by which management at every level can judge the results of its efforts. Such standards are more significant at lower than at higher levels, because with every step up the hierarchy more figures are aggregated and more generalized standards used for comparison. Hence the importance rightly attached to breaking down indices of control by standard costs and other means, to give guidance to the supervisor on the shop floor as well as to the directors in the board-room.

It is unhappily inescapable that the standards thus used to measure what 'ought to be' are estimates, based on a whole pyramid of assumptions. And when performance deviates from expectation, it is always a question whether the fault lies with the performance or with the estimates. All managers know by experience that control is possible only under conditions which are not always present. It must be possible to observe what is and to estimate what ought to be with some precision and without too much delay; and even when this is possible, the disparity does not always yield guidance in the next move. So the norms and limits which govern the conduct of a business – the standards of what ought to be and what ought not to be, whether in financial economic, social or any other terms – are estimates, hypotheses, assumptions, more or less conscious. Beneath them lie the realities I mentioned earlier – the economic and social laws which must be obeyed if the undertaking is to continue. But what operates to control the behaviour of management at all levels is the current set of standards as to what is to be expected. It is these which tend to be taken for granted but which need continual revision.

If the controls show that the man-hours consumed by a particular process are more than they should be, it is fairly easy to find and remedy the trouble. But even if they show that these are all they should be, it may still be true that the process itself has become inept and wasteful; that, though technically it is admirable, economically or perhaps socially speaking, it is a major source of inefficiency. The controls do not readily disclose their own shortcomings, and this is one of the reasons why it is easier to develop new skills and responses than to change the norms and limits by which these are measured.

I can now get a little nearer to defining what I mean by norms in the control of a business. They include all those standards by which efficiency is measured but which are not themselves similarly controlled. A change of method to satisfy the same criteria is merely an improvement in what I have called responses and skills; but a change in the criteria themselves is more difficult. It is also more important, for it is by such changes that major adaptations are usually made.

Consider now the operation of negative control, a process equally familiar both in mechanical and in organizational situations. The pressure gauge on the boiler is paralleled by the daily statement of the case position.

176

Negative control differs from positive control in important ways. First, it is intermittent; for it remains inoperative until the factor measured, be it steam pressure or overdraft, approaches the danger limit, whereas positive control is virtually always in action, since no norm is ever held precisely or for long. Again, it usually gives less directional guidance for there are usually more ways away from a danger than there are routes to a goal. Finally, and most important, the rightness of negative control is not verified by experience in the same way as positive control.

A man who steers on a given course for long enough will find out in the end whether the course itself was well chosen; but a man who consistently avoids a limit will never have the chance to learn by experience what would have happened if he had disregarded it. As a result we are bedevilled by bogus limits more often and for much longer than by bogus norms. For example, a restrictive practice, whether by workmen or employers, may or may not have had a valid origin, but as long as it persists there will be no opportunity to verify by experience whether it is still valid.

Briefly, then, I suggest to you that a business is a process controlled by a set of expectations, positive and negative, conscious and unconscious. This is the sort of firm we are and this is the sort of thing we do. These are the ways in which we are accustomed to act and these are the standards of performance we regard as satisfactory. These, on the other hand, are things we regard as unacceptable. You will not find these norms and limits written down in full in any rule book; the more important ones are unconsciously taken for granted. None the less, it is they which govern the behaviour of the undertaking; and its success depends on how closely these standards of what ought and ought not to be correspond with the world of reality in which the undertaking works.

Whence come these norms and limits? They are evolved by experience. Businesses, like individuals, are often hampered or even destroyed by unconsciously refusing to bring their norms and limits into line with the realities of the outside world; such refusals are the non-adaptive, 'neurotic' responses. But without neurotic refusal, a business,

177

like an individual, may still fail to adapt its norms and limits sufficiently wisely or swiftly to secure its own success or even survival.

It is useful, then, to distinguish two aspects of management's responsibility for adaptation. It has the responsibility of control, meaning by this the comparison of performance with standard at every level, without which operations are blind. But it has also the responsibility for continually revising the standards themselves, even when this involves abandoning sanctified goals and violating ancient taboos. And in this last function it has to be sensitive to the time factor, which limits what changes can be achieved in any given time without disrupting internal or external coherence beyond the threshold of what can be borne. And since this time factor is itself a function of the internal relationships of the organization, a major responsibility of management in a time of rapid change is to organize the undertaking so as to be adaptive.

Adaptation is a response of the whole system; it cannot be dictated from the board-room. Chester Barnard,[1] first observed that it is not the job of the brain to manage the body. The brain is part of the body; it depends on the body. The body has many functions which the brain can only confuse, and others which it is glad to decentralize to the level of reflex action as soon as it can. Its great function is to organize experience, so as to make possible complex and harmonious responses by the whole organism to changing situations over prolonged periods of time. This is equally the function of management. The management team, like the brain, is an integral part of the organization which it controls, widely diffused through it and dependent on it.

If adaptation is a response of the whole system, the human beings at each level of the hierarchy must make their own adjustments to the need for change. It follows that each part of the organization must be adaptable and that the challenges which reach each part must be such as to evoke the right response. Obviously this is a condition most hard to attain.

For each part of the organization is itself a system and is governed by its own norms and limits which are not necessarily those of the larger whole. The change in technique which presents itself to management as an improvement in efficiency may appear to the craftsman on the shop floor as a depreciation of the value of his skill. We are all familiar with these chameleon repercussions, which are so hard to foresee. And we tend to think of three ways to sceure acceptance of change planned in the board-room. We can present it as the only way to avoid disaster; or as a contribution to the good of the whole, which should come before that of any of its parts; or just as something which has to happen. Even taken together, these are often inadequate.

Adaptive responses are needed long before disaster is apparent, long before any one can prove with certainty that the response commended is the only one or even the best. Management is under great temptation to write up the threats it foresees from its vantage tower, in order to quicken response at lower levels. It is a dangerous temptation, to be strongly resisted. Men become habituated to the prophecy of doom, especially if it never happens; and they do not assume that it would have happened, but for the wisdom of their masters.

It is equally mistaken in my view to expect every employee of an undertaking to identify himself with its 'efficiency' to such an extent that this will operate on him and his group as a norm, not merely as a limit. To the work study man, the methods engineer and the production engineer, efficiency in terms of more results for less effort is an inspiring norm; but that is because their own success is bound up with it. To others it is unexciting – properly so, I think; and, though men resent doing obviously wasted work, they are much more ready to take pride in producing the superlatively good than the superlatively cheap. Maybe this is an attitude which could and should be changed. I doubt it. Much inhumanity has been wrought in the not so distant past in the name of efficiency and I doubt if it will be reinstated in our time as a norm with which every man on the shop floor can be expected to identify himself. It will remain a limit. What the producer accepts, whether in wages or conditions, will be conditioned by his idea of what the traffic will stand. But in our increasingly integrated and managed economy this is a matter on which economists and plain men find it equally easy to disagree, and management has to live down a century's reputation for being a biassed and unreliable witness on the point.

Finally comes the vexed question: how far should we rely on authority to dictate the need and the direction of adaptation? To consider this we need a definition of authority. I find most useful the one used by Chester Barnard and adopted by Herbert Simon.[2] Whenever some one accepts the decisions of another as his own without verifying them from their original premises, a relation of effective authority exists between the one and the other. This relation, as Simon points out, may hold in any direction; it is not limited to the one-way channels in which the chain of authority is depicted on an organization chart. The executive who leaves to his secretary a decision about filing cabinets is accepting her authority to that extent.

There is no doubt that authority in this sense is essential to the running of every organization. There is neither time nor opportunity to check and re-check the decisions of others, on which every one continually acts. This acquiescence must come either from trust or from indifference or because the decision is acceptable on other grounds, which the acceptor can verify.

I have been present at a number of meetings at which policy decisions of great importance to workers have been explained to them – such as the closing of a coal-mine. The chief value of these meetings has lain not in exposing logical arguments which were not clear before but in bringing together the policy-makers and those whom their policy affects, and thus giving the opportunity for trust to be generated. This to my mind is more than half the value of consultation and is the answer to the often heard criticism that it is no use consulting when those consulted are not able to add anything to the matter under discussion.

To promote adaptation at every level, then, one must first understand what are the governors of activity at the level concerned, the norms it tries to hold, the limits it strives to avoid. These must be won over to the change, or adpatation at that level will be sluggish or disruptive or successfully resisted.

The structure and culture of British industry is in many ways inimical to adaptation. First, I have in mind the time lag, increasing and perhaps bound to increase still further, which separates the sensing of the need for a change of policy from the earliest day when the new response can be effective. We must begin to act sooner, if we are not to be too late. Mass production is committed to a path which it takes some years to change. And this tendency to rigidity is made worse by the fact that the development of techniques proceeds ever more rapidly.

Again, for Britain, foresight must deal with more unpredictable variables, because of our dependence on world markets, both for our exports and for the imports of materials on which our exports depend.

Even more formidable perhaps are the rigidities which structure the human situation, such as the physical immobility of labour and the increasing tendency for wage and salary negotiations to be conducted nationally. This not merely fits individual firms to the Procrustean bed of the national average but it also removes the responding mechanism still further from the challenge which should move it to action.

Finally, we must count the inherited legacies of the past, abating perhaps but still strong, which create resistance to change at a time when even the greatest readiness may be insufficient to secure survival. Coupled with this is the eclipse of those indices which once signalled the need for change both to masters and men: the indices of the market.

The movement towards collective security is a natural and proper one, in the industrial and in the social sphere. Its danger is not ethical or psychological but practical. We are accustomed to respond, not to things we foresee, still less to things which others foresee, but to things which happen to us. If we screen these happenings from ourselves and remit the duty and the power of response to others at some remote level, we cut away the conditions on which speedy adaptation has hitherto depended.

To sum up the thoughts I have put before you, I suggest that the challenge which faces British industry over the next decades is a challenge of adaptation, and I have tried to give a fairly precise meaning to that familiar word. It is a challenge to achieve not merely a different relationship but a much more complex one. Internally, the individual undertaking is required to satisfy a wider series of demands. Externally, it is required not merely to keep afloat in more difficult water than before but to accept to a greater extent the demands which flow from being a more closely integrated part of the national economy. And in meeting these dual requirements it has a number of growing and inescapable handicaps.

Against this sombre outlook, we can set the fact that we have a better understanding of what adaptation means and of how management can speed it. We are accustomed to think of adaptation as the devising of new means to attain our ends or even as the choosing of new ends; but I have suggested that this traditional distinction between means and ends is inadequate for our purpose. The governors of behaviour for men and societies, as for all other open systems, are rather what I have called norms and limits – relationships between processes which must be maintained through time and thresholds beyond which these relationships must not be allowed to stray. These relationships are fairly familiar to us in economics but they are equally real in terms of social relationships and of personal dynamics.

The adaptation required of business during these critical decades will in my view involve not merely learning new responses and new skills but changing our norms and limits – the hardest of all adaptations. In particular it will involve adopting new criteria of success and of failure – and these in turn will derive from the need to acknowledge a much greater measure of mutual interaction and *inter*dependence, both between the individuals and groups which compose the organization and between the organization and those larger organizations, be they national, international or supranational, to which it must become increasingly bound by ties of participation and even obligation.

Paradoxically, one of the most valuable lessons which management can draw from current ideas of adaptation is the limitation of its own field. Its function is not so much to adapt as to maintain an organization which will be adaptive. Its most important utterances are in the indicative, not the imperative mood.

It is here, perhaps, that the changing concept which I have been pursuing shows most clearly. Traditionally, the manager is a commander and a leader. He says what shall be and he sees that it is so. He makes decisions and by authority he makes his decisions effective. This simple model, reduced to an absurdity which is not always remote from the actual, may lead management at each level to seek the greatest freedom from those above and the greatest authority over those below. It is a model acceptable only in days of small-scale enterprise and then only so long as the process of decision is hedged about with mystery.

Over against this concept, we can set another, which is coming into being and is more appropriate to our time. The question of who makes a decision is still important but less so than the question of who contributes its premises. Channels of communication become more important than chains of command. The organization as a whole is viewed not as a machine for executing the will of those at the top but as a quasi-organism, in which every part is engaged all the time in contributing to the inner and outer adjustments which its need as a whole requires.

Where does this leave our traditional concept of leaders and leadership? It leaves them, I suggest, debunked but not destroyed – stronger, indeed, for being purged of some outdated lumber. The faculty we call good judgment remains a precious one and those who show that they possess it in a high degree will, I am sure, continue to command the respect and the position they command now. Similarly, the power to convince others, to win and keep their trust in a world where so much more must be taken on trust, remains a precious faculty; and the combination of these two will, I fear, remain rare, though I believe that both can be developed to a degree greater than we yet realize by reducing the impediments which now prevent most men from using them to their full capacity.

On the other hand, these are qualities which are needed in some degree at every level of activity from top to bottom. It is part of every one's role to trust, as well as to win trust, to follow as well as to lead. Leaders and followers are not classes of men; they are functions spread through society in different proportions. Management in the future will have less room, at the one extreme, for the human cog and the human rubber stamp. Equally it will have less room for the pompous pundit and the manic boss. And in both respects it will be the better.

REFERENCES

[1] Barnard, Chester J. *The Functions of the Executive*. (1938) Cambridge, Mass.: Harvard University Press.

[2] Simon, H. A., *Administrative Behaviour*. (2nd ed. 1959) New York: Macmillan.

CHAPTER TWELVE

Background to Management*

IT SEEMS to me that two facts and the interaction of their results determine the major problems both of government and of management today. One fact is economic and relates to our situation in the world; the other is psychological and concerns our attitudes and aspirations, but it is just as much a matter of fact. The state of a man's mind, said an eminent judge, is as much a fact as the state of his digestion – as much a fact, he might have added, as the state of his bank balance. It is well known that the state of a man's bank balance can have a shocking effect on his state of mind and it is equally true that his state of mind can have a shocking effect on his bank balance. And this is relevant to what I have to say, because the two facts which I have in mind might be described very roughly as the state of our national bank balance and the state of our national mind. I will call them, respectively, *the siege economy* and *the welfare state of mind*.

The first fact which I have in mind is that during our lifetime the economic stability of this country has declined to a startling degree and that the causes of this decline are still in full force and are unlikely to abate for many years. I need not rehearse at any length the causes of this decline. For some decades of the nineteenth century we enjoyed a pre-eminence, in some fields almost a monopoly, in the arts of turning raw materials into manufactured goods. Raw materials were abundant, the accumulations of capital and skill needed for manufacture were scarce, and, as pioneers in the field, we reaped the benefit of their scarcity. We multiplied our population five times in one hundred and fifty years; raised our standard of living for the few and took it as our

*An address given at the annual conference of the British Institute of Management in 1952.

target for the many; and became dependent on the rest of the world for half our food.

Meantime, the monopoly passed and some of the natural advantages on which the pre-eminence was based, the early importance of coal, for example, in the world's carrying trade, dwindled in importance. Other manufacturing nations arose, their later start being in some ways an advantage rather than a handicap; and each addition to the world's manufacturing power increased still further the power to expand manufactures both there and elsewhere. For many years this power has been increasing faster than our power to increase the production of natural resources, even if we include the power to bring new raw materials into use. The pressure of rising populations tilts the balance still further in favour of primary and against secondary production.[1] We share with other manufacturing nations the loss of a differential advantage, in addition to losing our particular advantages over them. The terms of trade move on the whole against us, we have to export today nearly twice the value in manufactures which would have sufficed in 1938 to secure the same return in raw materials, and we are warned that this deterioration is bound to go on. We shall be stemming the tide for the rest of our lives, and if we are to hold our own with those whom that tide now favours or even to avoid being carried backwards on to the rocks, it can only be by virtue of some differential in our favour created by our own energy and skill.

I do not think that this is yet generally felt. Its first impact on the public mind I would date from that day in 1931 when we 'went off gold'. There may be, even in this distinguished gathering, some who are too young to remember the shock of shame and alarm which shook the country then, the instant urge to put right at once so gross a departure from the established order of the world. Well, we are a little more used to such things now; but collectively we are not, I think, fully aware of what has come to us, still less of what is coming. The war, which has speeded this decline, has masked its true nature.

The result of all this which particularly interests me tonight is the increase in planning and in policy-making and in control. This is inevitable in a 'siege economy'. Whenever anything becomes so scarce

186

that its distribution cannot be left to the market, someone is saddled with an inescapable responsibility for settling priorities. Who shall buy what with our limited foreign exchange? Who shall make what with our limited timber and steel? Deliberate policy must decide the answers; deliberate control must enforce them. As a result management has increasingly to reckon with the decisions of the Government and its agencies, instead of, or as well as, with the trends of markets, the yield of harvests and the credit of customers.

This tendency affects relations not only between industry and Government but also throughout industry itself. A siege economy makes policy more dominant, control more anxious and pervasive; and the effect is much the same whether an industry is organized as a single corporation, like the coal industry, or whether many units, still formally independent, co-ordinate their policies through an association. Standardization, to take a simple example, can bring savings in money and labour and material; and in these days these savings are important enough to become a matter of national concern. It claims much attention in the nationalized coal industry; but I gather that it claims even more in the non-nationalized automobile industry.

Even when, as with standardization, the advantages of 'co-ordination' are obvious, we all view the process itself with a suspicious eye, alert to attack bureaucracy, centralization and other such sinister growths; but we should not deceive ourselves about the result. If nothing were ever decided one single level higher than the lowest which would do; if no 'return' ever called for a single piece of information which was not really wanted; if no committee ever sat unfruitfully, or reported unnecessarily or advised ineffectively; above all, if no one were ever asked to conform with anyone else about anything without good and sufficient cause, even in that perfect world, we should still find ourselves being 'co-ordinated' much more than we ever were before.

A siege economy demands more solidarity, makes more demands on undeveloped loyalties, assumes a common understanding and a common will which only the demand can create. It thus provokes conflicting responses and breeds the frustration which is their inescapable, though, let us hope, their temporary result.

Frustration is a sign of the times and a sign which is easy to misread. You have probably noticed the curious fact that many Englishmen will accept a much worse deal from Providence than they will from their fellow men or at least from any of their fellow men with whom they stand in any sort of relationship. If they are ruined because the bottom falls out of a free market, they may possibly blame themselves, but they will at least blame no one else. But if they are even mildly mulcted by the award of some price-fixing body, they are likely to feel a deep sense of indignation. They can accept stoically the uncertainties and unfairness of an uncontrolled world but they cannot accept without fury the shortcomings and vagaries of a controller, even though in sum his results are more good than bad. This seems to me both odd and important and if it were a permanent shortcoming of human nature, the outlook would be sombre; so let us hope that it is due, as I believe, rather to the fact that those who feel this way have not yet learned to digest these new experiences as well as they can digest the old familiar ones.

Happily we can most of us call to mind 'combined operations', whether in peace or in war, in which groups of men, dispersed, exhausted, ill-informed, have none the less managed to carry out a common plan. I recall an offensive in France in 1915, carefully planned, elaborately rehearsed – it failed. I recall other operations three years later, more difficult, far less prepared, which succeeded. The men engaged were not better or better trained. Things went wrong just as often, but the organization had developed the power to put them right. Something subtle and unexplained had happened. There had come into being among all levels of command a mutual understanding not wholly dependent on the telephone. The same relationship was most aptly described in a recent article on training for management, in which the author declared that one of the chief tasks of management is to create a climate in which the staff and the work-people tend to do the right thing without being told. He was speaking of a medium-sized business; my illustration is drawn from an army in the field and I am talking about the relationship which we want to animate a community of fifty million people; but whatever the scale, the relationship required is in essence the same.

If men are to accept common direction without harm to their springs of energy and intiative, there must exist between them a particular kind of mutual rapport. Frustration is the sign of its absence and it is a danger signal. The remedy is either to relax the intensity of the direction or to increase the sensitiveness of the rapport. If, as I believe, the siege economy prohibits the first, the second becomes the more important – especially if, as seems clear, we do not really know what this rapport is or how we can build it up.

Reflecting then on the effect of the siege economy, I am led to conclude that it is bound to land us in a situation which will make great demands on our imaginations and our morals, as well as on our brains; because the task of adapting ourselves to new relations with people is an imaginative and a moral test, not merely an intellectual exercise. I conclude, too, that this is the aspect of organization which is likely to try us most highly and that it constitutes a major and all-pervading problem for management today, a double problem, for there is no level of management which is not also in some degree being managed.

I would not attribute this demand for closer rapport exclusively to the *siege economy*. It stems in part from the sheer growth in size of industrial units, which has been a feature of the whole industrial age and which would of itself have set us the same problem in the end, though more slowly. I agree also that our collectivism did not begin as an effort to close the dollar gap. Dicey, writing in 1905, dated the beginning of collectivist legislation at 1856, on the occasion when the House of Commons for the first time threw out a bill for enclosing a common and thereby registered the opinion – rank heresy at that date – that at least that bit of our English heritage was better left in common ownership. Three years earlier the present Lord Samuel had written a book to explain why the Liberal Party has abandoned unqualified *laissez-faire* in favour of such collective projects as accessible higher education and publicly provided housing. Neither Dicey the old-fashioned Whig, nor Samuel the new-fangled Liberal, based their views on the country's impending bankruptcy. Nothing was further from the thoughts of either. To Samuel in 1902 and to many like him the perplexing portent of their time was that in the richest country in the world a fifth of the population were too poor to keep themselves in health. The Welfare State can trace its lineage further back than 1902 and its developments had begun to quicken the pace of national integration, with all its strains and rewards, long before the economic blizzard brought its chilly emphasis. The fact remains that the economic controls which today co-ordinate British industry and set so many of its problems are products of the siege economy and that the policies which are effected through those controls are policies aimed primarily at economic defence and economic survival.

Yet the Welfare State supplies the second of those basic facts from which I began. I am concerned not with its substance but with the state of mind which it connotes.

The Welfare State connotes a demand by the citizen for security; for status; and to a less extent for opportunity. The character and emphasis of these demands was generated over the last hundred years by way of reaction to the experiences of that time; they crystallized in the depression of the early 30's; they may well persist long after the circumstances of their birth have passed away. Any government in this country must do its best to satisfy this complex of aspirations and expectations; and any management must do likewise.

For the same citizens who press these demands on governments, make the same demands as workers on their employers. Indeed, they are more concerned with the life of the work-place than with the life outside. It is in the work-place that these demands matter most today; and it is there that they are hardest to meet.

Let me summarize the view which I have put before you. We face nationally an unfamiliar and dangerous situation and we bring to it a national state of mind formed in a situation which was very different. Our aspirations, our expectations and our fears are a response not to the situation we are in now, still less to the situation to which we can look forward but to a situation which we have left. These two facts and their repercussions, I have suggested, give to the problems of management today their peculiar emphasis and character. Our economic situation calls for a great increase in productivity and hence for quick adaptation and a rapid increase of effective energy, both mental and physical. At the same time it calls for more co-ordination of policy, greater attention to ends and closer economy of means, two demands which in themselves are hard to reconcile. This reconciliation is at present made harder by our psychological situation, if I may so describe it, which calls for a more assured status for each producer, more attention to the impact on him of each new decision, more consultation with him, more security for him, more leisure and a greater individual return for effort. At first sight this would seem to be a mental inheritance perfectly unsuited to our needs.

Yet I believe that it is at least a stage along the road to becoming the sort of community which we need to be, a community which is informed throughout by so great a capacity for sensitive response that it can meet without confusion or disruption the sort of challenges which are coming to us. Whether we shall achieve such a community in time, only time itself can show. But if we are still unprepared for the next ten years, we are at least better prepared than we were fifty years ago.

The great coal strike of 1893 was settled by the Foreign Secretary at a conference held at the Foreign Office. Seen from the 1950's it seems a strange choice of mediators. Was it prompted perhaps by the sense that here the two nations of which Disraeli spoke were at issue and that mediation between nations was a Foreign Office job?

Little more than fifty years later, the Foreign Secretary was himself a great trade union leader. We should not suppose on that account that the two nations have completely fused. They have not. But they are immeasurably nearer to fusion. Our attitude of mind is itself partly the product and partly the cause of that mutual penetration of two once separate worlds and as such it is precious past telling. For the task ahead is a task for one nation, not two. As two nations we should be doomed from the outset. As one we have a chance.

None the less, the welfare state of mind as it exists today has elements of danger. Chief among these is that it cushions the effect of national insecurity in the mind of the individual citizen and makes it harder for him to recognize or to respond to it. In a simpler economy the peasant knows whether his efforts are winning him a livelihood. He knows how much it is. He knows that it is not necessarily as much as his efforts 'deserve'. He knows that, whatever it is, he cannot both have his cake and eat it. All these homely truths are still true of our national economy, but they are not wholly true of any individual one of us. How are we to produce a national response to a national situation, if what is wanted is something different from the sum of our individual responses to our individual situations?

Fifty years ago it seemed a paradox that there should be so much individual insecurity within a situation which was nationally so secure. Today the paradox is reversed. How can we reconcile collective security with national insecurity? Fundamentally the paradox is, I think, unreal. The harder the times, the more important it is that the load shall be spread as it may best be borne, that such security as there is shall be fairly shared, that everyone shall count and that nobody shall be wasted. So we can say with truth that fundamentally a siege economy calls for a Welfare State, for these are the Welfare State's underlying objectives. The danger lies not in the Welfare State but in some aspects of the welfare state of mind. In a real siege, every citizen can see the besetting dangers and every private life is altered by it. In our situation it might be that the individual first felt the impact on his own life after the walls had been breached. Unless we can respond individually to a group situation, collective security will damp down our responses until they are too late.

Well, there are my two facts – the siege economy on the one hand, the welfare state of mind on the other. The roads from them have converged on a single problem. Both demand that we shall learn individually to respond to a situation much wider than the one which we can directly know. This is a most difficult and indeed unnatural thing to do.

You know how much has been talked and written about the passing of the old many-skilled craftsman and his replacement by the specialist or the semi-skilled man on the assembly line. The old craftsman, they say, was better placed, partly because he had more scope to plan, execute and finish a complete job and partly because he was more independent of other people. I have watched a Scottish quarryman working alone in the section of face allotted to him – his 'motion' in local parlance. He had his tools and unlimited stone, periodically blown down for him; and every week they came and took away the sets and kerbs and borders which he had made and paid him for them. He kept his own hours, worked at his own pace, waited for no man, hurried for no man, neither received nor gave an order . . . He was a perfect example of the type with whom we are accustomed to contrast the man on the assembly belt.

What is the essential difference which we instinctively feel and deplore? To appreciate the answer, we need to think of action as response to a situation. The satisfaction which we get from acting depends very much on how free we are to respond to the situation as we see it; and the effectiveness of our response depends on how adequate our appreciation is. My quarryman was completely free to respond as he pleased to every situation which arose; and he was aware intuitively of almost everything which he needed to know in order to respond effectively. He scarcely needed conscious thought. The same may be true of men working in a small team. But the man on the assembly line and the specialist whose work is part of a still wider synthesis tends to be pulled back, pushed on or pushed about by events to which he cannot effectively respond – the stoppage of the conveyor belt, for instance – or by decisions with which he cannot identify himself; and he needs a profound change of mind if he is to be happy and effective.

I remind you of the forces underlying this familiar problem, because it seems to me that something very similar is happening to management. The proprietor of the one-man business, like my quarryman, had the world for his oyster and was free to respond to it as he pleased. The manager of today is making part of a collective response to a situation wider than he can know and much wider than he can feel; and insofar as he does know the new features in this situation, they are often the harder to accept, because they seem irrelevant to his job.

Most of them stem either from the siege economy or from the welfare state of mind; and neither of them shows the slightest tendency to abate.

Consider another example from the coal industry. When Saturday work was re-started in the coal industry, much thought was given by people in the coalfields to the conditions under which a voluntary 'overtime' shift could be made to provide most coal. It was worth adjusting the length of the shift a little to enable men who started in early morning to get home in time to share the pleasures of Saturday afternoon. A few coalfields wanted to cut it by forty-five minutes more than the remainder. They knew their men and their conditions, their shift times, their kick-off times, all the rest of that local 'situation' and this was their 'response'. Unfortunately the length of the shift was one of those things – fewer than is sometimes supposed – which had to be common; so they could not have their way. It was very hard to convey to the men on the spot that on this occasion 'the people in London' were not ignoring the views of the men on the spot but that on the contrary they were accepting the views of men on many spots and that incidentally they were themselves on a 'spot' – perhaps in more senses than one. Yet it was of great importance that the people in the coal-fields should be so convinced; for otherwise there would be no rapport, no mutual response and hence a chilling of energy and a dimming of vision.

Clearly both managing and being managed are getting more diffi-cult and in at least three ways, all of which this little example illustrates. First, it is difficult to assemble all the relevant facts for these broad decisions. Next, it is more difficult still to make the decisions acceptable to those who are to act on them, I do not mean difficult to exact their obedience but difficult to get them to put into effect with the same lively initiative which they would put behind a response of their own. These are difficulties of communication. Finally, apart from difficulties of communication, there are difficulties inherent in the act of decision itself. The art of management includes the art of deciding, the art of being informed and the art of communicating – I call them all 'arts' advisedly – and all three are making new and greater demands.

My quarryman's decisions were barely conscious; he seldom needed to weigh the pro and con for the whole situation was present to him and his response was almost instinctive. So were mine when I practised as a lawyer; so are most of the responses of an independent manager, so long as the scale of his operations is not too big for him to apprehend his situation directly. But in industry today decisions have to be taken over a field too wide to be within the intuitive grasp of anyone. Even in policy making, therefore, we are up against the same difficulties which specialization always involves. No one enjoys either the satisfaction or the certainty of responding directly to the situation. The processes of rational decision have to be dragged up into the light of day. Intuitive assurance of what to do, which is the best sort of assurance, plays an ever-smaller part in major decisions and the part it does play becomes ever less helpful, for it tends only to exaggerate the importance of those parts of the situation which are intuitively known.

This provides us, I think, with an important bit of background to management studies. There is a point at which the scale of management changes its problems not only in degree but in kind. Men successful and experienced in what would have been called large-scale management thirty years ago have to learn new and irksome tasks when they come to what is large-scale management today. They have to learn to accept the limitations of remoteness, to learn the infinitely difficult art of helping to make up a collective mind instead of merely making up their own.

They have today some remarkable technical aids. The mechanical means now at our disposal for collecting, classifying and handling facts, especially facts which can be expressed as figures, already far exceeds our human abilities for using them. Computers will surely occupy ever more space in our offices. All these devices will give us the right answers, if we feed them with the right facts and ask them the right questions; but they do not help us with the two 'ifs' and they make it harder for us to proceed by trial and error, because they give a certain rigidity to the questions which they are set to answer. I have no doubt that top management in the future will have to know more than was expected of it in the past about the methods, the possibilities and the limitations of statistical science; but this in itself will not help us in deciding what questions to ask or, if you like, what indices to watch.

Here again times change. In a private undertaking the primary criterion of efficiency is whether it pays; and of this its accounts provide a clear and reliable index. In an undertaking with statutory duties, like the National Coal Board, the proper criterion of efficiency is to enquire how well it is doing the job which it was set up to do, having regard to all the circumstances. The duties of the Coal Board under its Act are not to make profits but to get the country's coal, to organize the industry and to make coal available to the consumer as may best serve the public interest as regards quantity, quality, size and price. How is the public – or the Board itself – to judge how well this duty is being performed? How are we to weigh the indices of output, of productivity, of cost, of price and with what standards are we to compare them?

I am tempted to pursue this a little further, because I think it is a point of no small importance that significant indices of control in the coal-mining industry are both different from what they were and more difficult to select and to interpret than they used to be. This would lead us to consider how under these new and exacting conditions we are to measure and to audit efficiency. That, however, would lead us into the foreground of management. I am concerned only to point out how real and how pressing this problem is – not only in the coal industry but also in many others on whose efficiency our wellbeing depends no less, even though their duties to society are not written in an Act of Parliament. For even in private industry over an increasing sector profitability is no longer an adequate index of the most efficient use of resources.

But there is much more in the art of communicating then merely passing information. The beginning of wisdom, as it seems to me, is to recognize that human communication has nearly always a double effect and usually a double object. When A and B talk, they may or may not learn something from each other but they certainly create or modify a mutual relationship and this relationship is primarily one of confidence or its opposite.

A man who spent part of the war in Fighter Control told me that the tone of voice was as essential to success as the speed and accuracy and relevance of the information passed. The fighter pilot, you may say, wanted information and nothing else; but it could only travel along a bond of human confidence.

What happens in the course of industrial consultation? Is its value measured by the information which is imparted? Is it not rather measured by the confidence which it creates? In the coal industry since Vesting Day we have closed one hundred and thirty-seven pits, for various technical reasons. We have offered more productive work elsewhere to most of the workers, so that output has not suffered; but each closure means the break-up of a social group, often with a long history; and each closure has meant hardship to some and disturbance for many. Each proposed closure has, of course, been the subject of full consultation. Only once has there been a stoppage of work; only five times has the closure not been agreed by all concerned without reference to headquarters.

On each of these five occasions the process of consultation was repeated at national level. Everyone came, from the colliery manager and the branch secretary to the National Board. The whole decision was reviewed.

So far as I know, nothing new was said on any of those occasions. Nothing, previously overlooked, emerged. Every fact and every argument had already been used at other levels. No information passed which had not passed before. I am not even sure that anyone changed his opinion. In all but one of these cases the final decision was the same as the original proposal.

Yet something happened in those cases, no less than in the one where a change was made. A decision, previously unacceptable, was accepted. There was a change, not in opinion, but in relationship and hence in attitude.

I turn in conclusion to a question which has been knocking ever more loudly for attention during this argument. I have invited you to agree that both the siege economy and the welfare state of mind call for a very high degree of co-ordination in our actions and consequently in

our understanding and our sympathy. I have pointed out that this requires us to share individually in forming a common view of the situation and in responding to it, in making up our collective mind and in
carrying out its decisions as if they were our own. The logic of all this
seems to me to be disagreeably cogent; but the still unasked question
is, have we any reason at all to suppose that human beings are capable
of building a relationship of this sort sufficiently strong and sensitive to
carry the sort of strain which, I have suggested, it needs to bear. The
answer, I think, is 'no'. I know of no community so large which has ever
succeeded in meeting a challenge of this order.

We should not on that account despair, but it is only common prud-
ence to make a realistic assessment of our resources. Efficiency experts
have been telling us for a long time that those who design new machines
should have regard to the capacities and limitations of the men who are
to use them; and they call in the doctors and the physiologists to say
what human beings can stand. It is high-time we applied the same
principles to managers. Unhappily, neither physiologists nor doctors
can yet say what managers can stand. And even when we can see what
they do not stand, we do not know whether this is some inherent
limitation of human nature or some lack of adjustment in themselves.
If I were talking foreground, I would discuss how the manager's job can
be made less difficult; but as I am talking background, I am free to
speculate on human limitations. For a third basic fact has emerged from
my pursuit of the other two. It is this: we have no assurance at all that
human nature is capable of the sort of collective response for which the
situation calls.

I sometimes think that we are in danger of inventing a *Social Man*
capable of doing almost as much damage in our day as the *Economic
Man* did in the days of our grandfathers. It is important, certainly, not
to think of men as things or as cogs in a machine; but it is equally
important not to think of them as gods or as cells in an organism. We
still tend to start from the assumption of man with all the rational
character that the nineteenth century gave him and then let the psychologists and the sociologists explain why he is neither so rational nor
so individualistic as on that showing he ought to be. I think we should

do better to start with the zoologists and speculate how it is that we humans are on the whole so much more socially adaptable than our fellow creatures and how we can best respond to this new and sterner challenge to adaptation.

I lately read with fascination the classic study[2] in which Professor Tinbergen describes his experiments and observations of animal behaviour and the conception to which they have led him. His descriptions were all too familiar; he could have observed large areas of my own behaviour and reached the same results. I think my fraternal feeling is strongest for the sticklebacks.

These creatures, it seems, in the breeding season take territories, like robins; and when two sticklebacks with adjacent territories meet on their common boundary, they behave in a very curious way. Since they do not know whether to fight or to fly, they do something which is related to neither and which is indeed altogether inappropriate to the situation. To be exact, they stand on their heads and dig holes in the ground.

Now territory fights are common in new organizations; in them Professor Tinbergen could observe behaviour very much like the stickleback, the same conflict of impulses, the same inability to produce a sensible response, the same irrational behaviour. None of us probably has ever seen two officials of different departments standing on their heads digging holes in the ground, but some of us may sometimes have wished that they would do something so relatively harmless, and I wish I was quite sure that no one could ever have wished the same for me.

If we look at behaviour throughout the animal world, we see the same picture constantly repeated. We see creatures producing beautifully apt and quick responses to the kinds of situation which they normally meet, yet thrown into utter confusion if the situation is unfamiliar or if it awakens two different responses at the same time. We see too, that situations are recognized by one or two conspicuous features rather than by their essentials, like the ducklings, described in a famous book[3] by another ethologist, Lorenz, which will accept as 'mother' any creature whatever which makes the right quack at ground level – even if it be the ethologist himself. We see the power of habits which have survived their usefulness to imprison the creature which they once served and often to bring it to destruction, by confining it to a definite sequence of responses. Well, this nature is part of our human heritage also. Men also tend to recognize situations by superficial labels and to respond to them by stock reactions. Men also are often ready to follow the wrong leaders in the wrong directions, so long as they make the same old quack. And is not the history of industrial relations littered with unhappy memorials to men who became imprisoned in 'a definite sequence of responses' by habits of mind forged how many years before?

Yet we have far outstripped the rest of the animate world in adaptability. How we do this is by no means clear; but it seems to include at least three processes. We come to understand our situation; we realize it imaginatively in our heads; and we respond to it, perhaps with as much liveliness as if it was before our eyes. This is magic indeed. It enables us sometimes, though rarely and with great difficulty, to break our own habits before they break us. We do not know how far this faculty can be developed; so we do not know for certain that the adventure on which we are embarked is impossible.

So it is worth trying to make it come true.

It is for this purpose that leading industrial undertakings both public and private are making so much more use of courses and conferences as part of management training at all levels from the foreman to top management. The power to reflect is not given us to beguile our leisure hours. It is the means and, I believe, the only means whereby we can keep ourselves alive in a world as difficult as the one which we are making for ourselves.

And there is encouragement in the history of the last generation. I am old enough to compare men of thirty with their fathers at the same age and I find the comparison very encouraging. (I know this is an odd and original view in one approaching sixty.*) I think they are on the whole far better equipped than their fathers for meeting the kind of challenge which I have described. Unhappily they have a bigger challenge to meet. If I am right, how have they learned to stand more firmly on the feet of reason, to see more deeply with the eye of imag-

*See footnote at the beginning of this chapter.

ination? This is the process which we must study and quicken and widen. It is a process most near to the purposes of this Institute.

For it seems that we are challenged to build up in our imaginations a picture of our common situation so lively and so accurate that we can respond to it willingly and effectively. We have to re-condition ourselves to respond differently to new situations, even though their conspicuous features do not change; and thus to change our habits, without losing them. We have to establish by these means a sufficient common element in our inner worlds to ensure that our responses will be coherent in themselves and consistent with those of others; and on this basis we have to build within industry and to the measure of its expanding needs a social relationship equally remote from the law of the jungle and from the law of the hive.

This is a whale of an objective; indeed, it may prove to be a Moby Dick. Alternatively, our experience may resemble rather that of a less ill-starred adventure than Captain Ahab's; that Nantucket whaler which returned from a three-year voyage without having sighted a whale at all. Her skipper's only comment was:

'*Well we've had a damn fine sail.*'

Perhaps the comment is less irrelevant than it sounds; for it may be that what we hunt is more important than what we catch.

But here I approach the background of a subject wider even than management.

NOTES AND REFERENCES

[1] Recent history has not confirmed this trend. The potential capacities of the undeveloped world, especially for organic products, may long postpone it. It seems to me none the less improbable that countries possessing surplusses of raw materials will operate much longer in a buyers market.

[2] Tinbergen, N., *The Study of Instinct*. (1951) Oxford University Press.

[3] Lorenz, K., *King Solomon's Ring*. (1952) London: Methuen.

Index

203

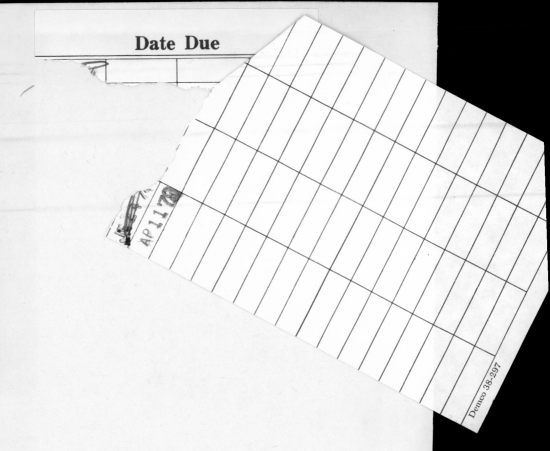